SOUL

SOUL
The Master Teacher

Sushil Bharti, O.P. Malhotra

KALPAZ

ISBN : 978-93-5128-071-2
Price : ₹ 240

First Published 2014

Published by

Kalpaz Publications
C-30, Satyawati Nagar,
Delhi-110052
Ph. : 9212142040
E-mail: kalpaz@hotmail.com

Laser Typesetting : Gyan Print (AB-II), Delhi
Printed at : G. Print Process, Delhi

Cataloging in Publication Data—DK
Courtesy: D.K. Agencies (P) Ltd. <docinfo@dkagencies.com>

Bharti, Sushil.
Soul : the master teacher / Sushil Bharti, O.P. Malhotra.
p. cm.
Includes index.
ISBN 9789351280712

1. Soul—Miscellanea. I. Malhotra, O. P., joint author. II. Title.

DDC 128.1 23

Contents

Preface

Have you ever thought about the soul?

Have you ever identified your soul?

Have you ever tried to know what the soul is?

Many of us do not know what exactly soul is. Though you have heard this word many a time in your life but you have not gone deep down to understand to identify our own soul. When I heard this word 'Soul' from Mr Malhotra, I started laughing and thought that now I will get to know something weird, that we have been hearing since our childhood about the soul. All sorts of scary stories related to soul and *Aatma* had been narrated many times by older people. For a moment, I was roaming in my past where imagination used to create a new world every time. Somehow, I managed to control my laugh and have listened Mr Malhotra with rapt attention.

To be very honest, as Film-maker, Novelist and a Storyteller whatever observations and experiences I had from my life, I never took soul as a serious subject earlier. For me, it was something that cannot be studied, something mysterious and unfathomable.

Mr Malhotra was living with this divine thought for the last 40 years and that was the total essence of his life. He had explained and gave reason to all my immature questions related to the soul. I suddenly found that soul-searching is the subject that I was looking for years. There are many questions that are still unanswered about life. I as a creative and sensitive person often used to argue with people and eager to know about life and death but never got satisfactory answers. When I did introspection and really surprised to know all my queries were connected to soul. After meeting with Mr Malhotra, gradually I got deeply involved to comprehend about soul and it changed my perspective completely towards life. I got all the answers that I was looking for so long related to soul. It was kind of a relief and mental peace, as if I got something that will give me peace, prosperity and a different perspective towards life. You may say a ray of hope to know yourself in and out completely. I really thankful to Mr Malhotra from core of my heart that helped me to understand about the soul as a subject in a real sense and inspired me to take a right path in life. You must be wondering that why I am saying right path, because earlier I was doing things according to the worldly pace but after meeting him I understood the meaning of soul and adopted the right path in life. Now, I feel this is the only way to get real happiness and high success in life.

Mr Malhotra was running a chit-fund company. He failed miserably in that business and virtually on the road. He had no idea what he would do next. A man whose future was in dark and top of that having a responsibility of seven members in the family was maddening. His mind was choked but his inner-soul guided him and he started another one after failing in chit-fund business.

He entered in 'bra'-making business. His mother, wife and three daughters got scandalised. According to them what the society and the close relatives will say? They won't be able to face people when they will ask all sorts of unusual questions that was the major concern of the family. Mr Malhotra was firm and confidant about his next venture that he will do bra-making business only. He had a strong feeling that one day he will be in a position to own his personal Merc-benz car. It was hard to believe to family members but he moved on. He started his journey in such an environment as a small entrepreneur again with the guidance of his soul. That firm determination and conviction bore fruit in the form of immense success that he has not dreamt in his life ever.

He has shared his unique experiences and success story and told clearly about whatever success he has achieved, it is because of his soul only, nothing else. It was really an indeed a unique experience hearing him on soul subject. He always speaks through his heart. He often says "whatever you want to say, say it from your heart and it will inspire others also to speak from their heart". He always wanted to share his success and this divine thought among people that soul is everything. It is the root cause of everything good and soul will definitely and always warn you about bad things. He strongly believes, if you will identify your soul, your life will be fulfilled with peace and happiness forever. According to him it is God's will and this divine thought should reach to the masses. As he got the benefit of this divine thought he thinks, let the people should also get the same advantage. Actually, that was the beginning of this book and it started taking a new shape.

I want to clarify one thing to all my readers that whatever thoughts and experiences we have woven in this book are representing Mr Malhotra's ideology. He strongly believes in these thoughts and follows them with great conviction and firm determination. He has been living with these thoughts for so long, he had thought over it many times, experienced it, proved and found logic for every single thought that has been described in this book. As a writer, my role is confined to give these thoughts an appropriate meaning and introduce my readers to soul in a simplest way.

I find myself really a fortunate writer, who got the chance to write such a wonderful book. It will be our great victory if it could bring improvements in awareness and self-confidence in people's life. We did our level best to put every factual thoughts and easy to understand in an interesting manner in this book. Our aim is people should try to identify their own soul which is their inner being and the most important element in their body and bring a positive change in their life. Create a solid vision and mission in life to achieve higher success in an ethical and authentic manner with peace of mind.

Soul is spiritual, immortal, living and infinite. And there is God's special element in you. It is a noble way to find ecstasy and spirituality in life. Soul is the only way to find immense and real success. All the great people of this world have identified their soul, connected with soul, and developed a beautiful relationship with their soul. They have heard the voice of their soul and acted according to the directions of their soul and achieved stupendous success.

This book is dedicated to all my friends who are misguided, misled and have not found their right path on the way to their success. Whole life they have been doing wrong things, took wrong direction and have not reached anywhere in life. Consequently, they have not achieved anything in life, felt cheated, deserted, frustrated, unsatisfied and disappointed. Though they have live full-life, done hard work but have not reached anywhere. They have not got chance to live with peace and happiness for a single day. Whatever effort they have done, have gone waste. Now, they do not have any aim and objective in life. Their monotonous life has taken a different route where no one can feel satisfied.

In such a state of mind, living a life has got no meaning at all. They have lost the meaning of self-respect, self-esteem, self-confidence and conviction. In the rat race of earning money, they have lost the track and the real meaning of life and its aim. Failure leads to fear and they are caught up in various rituals and astrological beliefs. They always tried to achieve inferior gain. And the result is now they are leading a painful life that they do not wish to lead. They are still unaware about the power of the soul.

This book will give a new dimension and logic to those, who have still not identified their inner-being, the soul. It will help people to understand and indentify their soul in real sense, so that they can change their life forever with peace of mind and positive attitude.

Soul cannot be seen. No one can touch it but surely can feel it. For instance, you cannot see love, air and electricity. Likewise, you cannot see soul. We can clearly see its result and affect. The body is lifeless and soul is the power for action. Every part of the body can be seen, one can feel also. But these parts cannot perform automatically. They need instructions to perform. Only the soul can plan good action. It gives information to people about bad things. People can follow those instructions and perform accordingly. In a nutshell, due to soul our body is alive. Otherwise, without the soul body is lifeless. The body cannot do anything by its own. When any human being died, according to Hindu culture, we say *Arthi* means dead body. When we add words "Sa" before *Arthi* it becames *Sarthi* without this *Sarthi*, body becomes lifeless if you ignore the instructions of soul you are worst than a dead body.

You must have heard various words related to *Aatma* like *Dusht-atma, Pret-atma, Dev-atma, Punay-atma*. The real owner of your body is soul rest are its employees.

Generally, it has been noticed when owner is not in the office, entire office atmosphere becomes arbitrary because no one is there to control the workers. Same goes with soul also, if the soul is not identified in that case illness, jealousy, dishonest, deceive all these factors lead your life. As a result, you become slave of these bad habits and cannot achieve good things in life.

This book introduces us to the real owner of the body and its functions. You must have familiar with all those great people who have identified their soul much early in their life got highly successful and served the humanity as a whole. The soul has got enormous power to identify your ability to choose right profession and business to become No. 1 in your field that you have chosen according to the soul's instruction.

While writing this book, we tried our level best that every topic should be easy to understand. If our readers will find that can make a difference in their life then they should start implementing these thoughts in daily life. This book will help you to achieve mental peace and accomplishment. Apart from that, it will also help you to lead a healthy life, get mental peace and physical relief. It will also help you to get proper respect wherever you are working, be it in the office or home, among your colleagues and friends. This book will also be helping you to control your anger, bad habits, jealousy, revenge, family relations, unnatural sex, bad food habits and even extra marital relationships.

As far as the religious faith is concerned that have been discussed in the book. We have only written truth, nothing else. The intention behind these topics to make people aware and make them understand what is good and what is bad for them. Our main concern is to help people to understand the real meaning of God. How a person can make a true bonding with the God through his soul and make his life successful in real sense. We respect our readers. You may disagree with our thoughts. You may not like certain ideas. We respect your opinion completely. Our intention is very clear. We want every individual should become the part of human evolution and he or she should be contributing something to the humanity. He or she should bring the positive change in society and people's life. It is our strong belief that it can happen only through soul.

Sushil Bharti, O.P. Malhotra

1

Identify Your Soul

Constant Evolution

We all have born on this earth for constant evolution to contribute your bit for humanity. This is a process of evolution for 14 billion of years on this earth. We are a part of it. We all are aware that life cycle is mysterious. You take birth, live life and when grow old, and you change the body to take rebirth. It is the story of every human being whosoever is taken birth on this earth; you keep changing your dress and address. Without your soul, your body is lifeless. It has got no divine value but it has got its part value only if it is used for other living bodies with soul. Now, the question arises how this birth cycle works? Who does change your dress and address? The answer is it is your soul, who is living, mature, dynamic, creative, and spontaneous, changes his dress and address. Changing dress means, soul entering in a new body, address means, you take birth in some other place. It becomes your new address. That's how the cycle of life works and we all are integral part of it. This birth and death cycle is a universal truth and it exists since its inception and beyond your control.

Soul Identification

In this chapter, we are going to discuss about the soul identification. How a person can identifies his soul and work accordingly. You must have observed, generally you do not hear the inner-voice of your soul. It gives you instruction, it raises objections, it warns you but you ignore it, though it is important to hear your soul carefully. Why it happened? Why don't you hear your soul's voice? Why do you do that? Have you ever thought of it? Let's find out this question. Why people ignore the voice of soul?

The acceptance of soul's massage needs control on your easy-going life. It becomes your habit and you feel that this easy-going habit is right. That is the reason you don't listen to your soul, moreover, you give example of others who are part of this easy life and always try to justify that what is wrong in it when everybody is involved and enjoying.

Temptation and Greed

You must have noticed in today's world that people have become self-centered and govern by various temptation and greed. You want to earn more and more money and want to be a highly successful person. Even you earn money through unethical means without realising it consequences. What you are doing and why? In the rat race of becoming successful and to earn more and more you divert from the right path and compromise with your self-respect. You become the part of the outer world and act like the majority of people are doing today. You become the part of crowd and start behaving in the same manner, where there is no mind, no peace, no real success, only confusion and chaos in life.

Here we want to clarify one thing that if you must hear the inner voice/the soul, build-up an honest relationship with God and will act according to the soul's voice, you will get true happiness, peace, prosperity and real success in life.

First of all you must know yourself and then choose your work according to your ability, interest and knack. If your mind, heart and soul harmoniously to do that specific work, it means what God has specifically chosen for you has been identified. You should take it as "God's *Prasadam*". It is a gift from almighty. When you work in that direction the success is sure, no one can stop you by getting immense and unbelievable success in your life and that will be the true and real success. In another words, God has sent you on this earth to do that specific work only. He has not created you similar to others, you are special for him and that is why you look different from others with specific likes, dislike and professional knowledge. So, it is obvious that God has chosen a specific or different job for you. It means, it is essential for you to find out your hidden work area and by adopting it you can serve to the humanity. Now it is up to you, how you are going to identify that particular work which is for you only but is not possible without identifying your soul. That particular work has got some kind of connection from your last birth and that knowledge of work come along with your birth in your new life. You need to identify or rectify that intellectual capacity by knowing your soul. But generally we do not identify or we may say that we do not try to identify that right job for us.

You often meet people by saying that "I don't know what is going to happen in my life?" I don't know what should I do? "Look at that fellow what was he earlier?" And where he is today? Whatever business I have tried, it failed. Only God knows when he will hear me and bless me? You put blame on God. The almighty God has designed a system, a path, a noble principle to get real success in life. One will have to follow that path with utmost sincerity then only things will work out in right direction.

I will give an example to clarify this. Suppose, you are a father of two sons. Elder one is Aasharam and he is 20 years old and the younger one is Satyaprakash and he is 18 years old. You often notice Aasharam is dishonest; he has habit of telling lies. He hides things. He takes responsibility half-heartedly and doesn't fulfill. He has his own world that he doesn't share with anybody. Whereas the younger son Satyaprakash is very much open, kind-hearted, understanding, he is honest and sincere. He would like to spend time with family and he is a responsible person. You do your own business. One day, there is an urgent need of five-lakh rupees. You call your wife and tell immediately send someone to the bank and withdraw five-lakh rupees. Your wife asks you whom should she send to the bank Aasharam or Satyaprakash? You think for a moment and says "Satyaprakash" now the question is why Satyaprakash? Why not Aasharam? Because you find that Satyaprakash is capable and sincere to do this job and will take full responsibility. It is his good image and character. Just think for a moment, if you can't trust your own son and taking decision in favour of suitable candidate, then how can you think that God will hand over the responsibility to someone just like that? He will also see whether the person is suitable for that work or not. Is he on a right track? Is he competent enough to take the responsibility? If you want to get high success then you have to follow the right path and right principles. You should be truthful and honest. You have to prove your mettle then only God will embrace you and handover the responsibility that will lead towards your desired goal.

Divine Connection

God is not going to do anything until you take initiative and start knowing yourself in and out. If you want to do something in your life then you must know your soul. You need to develop a divine connection with your soul. You have to be friendly with it. You need to hear its voice clearly. You need to follow its instruction. We all get instructions from soul time to time but do not follow them rather ignore them. We do not work according to those instructions. The soul will do its sense of duty. It will keep instructing you till your last breath. It is up to you whether you take it or leave it.

The soul is powerful and dynamic. When you see something bad is happening around you. You are disturbed and often say, 'no... no'... I will not support this matter. This should not happen. My conscious does not allow me to become a part of this. You take a decision to keep away yourself from that matter.

Swami Vivekananda beautifully described soul in his words:

"You have to grow from inside out. None can teach you, none can make you spiritual; there is no other teacher but your own soul."

"With your birth, God has sent you to play some role on this earth. You have to perform your role. Like an actor plays a role in movie and theater. The day when you will identify your definite role or work, you will not indulge yourself in other activities. You will concentrate only on your part that God has chosen for you specifically. Now, you must have got the answer why people say, "I do not know when God will bless me".

Here, I want to share one interesting instance with you. A lawyer got interested in film-making. He met one director and expressed his desire that he wants to make a movie. Director understood his concept and told that movie can be made on that subject. Suddenly, lawyer said "he will write the script". The director was shocked but lawyer convinced him that he knows the subject and he will do the justice to the script. The director also thought that let him do since he is aware about the subject and as far as the technicalities of the script is concern, he will see it later.

Work started, somehow they could manage to write an unprofessional and unconvincing script, reason being, lawyer was not ready to listen. He was adamant and not allowing any new thoughts and creative approach. Anyway when the script part was over suddenly one-day lawyer announced that he will act in the movie. Director was not in that favour but he said yes, why because the lawyer was financing the movie. The height of the drama was, lawyer started performing as a director on the set and it was difficult to handle him. It was totally unexpected and considering the situation it was bound to happen. The future of the movie was in dark and it was expected exactly the same, the director was predicting right from the beginning. Director had to stop the movie in the middle and move out from that funny situation.

Actually, it happened because director could not follow his principle and he should not accept that work without a complete script with the specific objective of the film. The director could have said straight away no to the lawyer for his unprofessional attitude. Here, we need to understand the director as he could not follow his principle and the producer has unprofessional attitude because of that they had to leave the project in the middle and lost their relationship forever.

If we assess this situation clearly both of them were at fault. They should speak through their heart and soul. That was not lawyer's work, then why he was getting into it. He was a big lawyer at one point of time. He has also got immense success in his life. God has blessed him as a lawyer. In a nutshell, you should not interfere in somebody's work because that is not for you, if it would have belong to you then you would have been doing that only, nothing else. Every job is not for everyone. You have to choose your job or work according to your ability and the voice of your soul.

In another example, a television serial director used to act in front of actors before commencing the scene to make them understand what the scene is all about. The job of the director should be to get into the scene and explain to the actors to perform accordingly rather than performing the role in front of them and asked them to do it like that only. In that process, many senior artists got offended and left the shooting in between. According to actors they are an artist and will give the performance according to the character's demand, if that is not appropriate then the director should guide them. Explain the requirement of the scene and they should get into that character and bring the appropriate emotions and expressions that are required for the scene. Now, you must have got an idea what we are trying to say. You should know your job and do it properly rather than getting into somebody else's cup of tea. You should be specific to your job. If you will follow this you will not be a mediocre. To become a successful personality in this world, your focus and concentration is must and that cannot come without knowing your soul.

Now, we will take some more examples from our society. The people who have heard the voice of their inner-soul trusted its power and identified that divine knowledge and guided his or her life according to that way they have achieved immense success and happiness in their life. Once those people have identified their path or right direction through the soul, they never looked back in life and got unbelievable success.

Self-realisation

One day the great sage Buddha, a divine soul, had a self- realisation and left everything behind, even his wife and son, all the luxury of his life. He became the ascetic, the *Sanyasi*. He found the root cause of human pain and sufferings. Budha sacrificed his materialistic life to achieve wisdom and truth and got an insight that if your desire will be less, you will live with peace and happiness forever. Ecstatically, he did all his effort in this direction and spreaded the message of divine knowledge to every human being that we should learn how to control our desires. If you will do that you will be free from all pain and sufferings of human life.

You must have heard the name of famous dacoit "Angulimal". He used to rob and murder people, cut their fingers and wear them in the form of garland. Have you ever thought why "Angulimal" become the disciple and followers of Budha? The Budha made him realise that whatever he was doing, it is an easy job. To destroy a human body, murdering someone physically is not a difficult task. This is the work that anybody can do it.

There is a beautiful story behind this:

Dacoit Anglumal : The people of Kushinagar was terrified and horrified due to tyranny of notorious dacoit Angulimal. *Mahatma* Budha decided to go to Angulimal. People told all sorts of horrendous stories about Angulimal. They dissuaded him that he should leave this idea to meet Angulimal since he was a very dangerous man. Budha was firm on his idea and he asked people, if he would not go to him then who would go? People did not have any answer of this loaded question. Finally, Budha went to meet Angulimal all alone. As Budha entered his premise, Angulimal warned him to keep away from him but Budha ignored his order and proceeded. He threatened Budha if he would come to him he would finish him. Budha did not mind it. He went and stood in front of him. Angulimal was furious. Budha simply asked him what you are you doing? He said arrogantly, can't you see what am I doing? Oh! I can clearly see what you are doing? "You just indulge in murdering innocent people, children and women", said Budha. He further added whatever you are doing it is a very easy task. After hearing this, Angulimal got more furious and said don't you know whom you are talking to? Budha said just take it easy way as I am yours, not to worry. First answer my question then do whatever you want to do with my body. Angulimal asked what is your question? Well, can you see that leaf on the tree? Angulimal answered 'yes. Go and get it, Angulimal went and cut the whole branch with his axe and gave it to Budha. He smiled and told, now go and put it back as it was. The moment Angulimal heard this, his mind was numbed. He was confused what to do. Budha again said go and replace that branch on the tree as it was before.

Angulimal was stunned and surrenderd himself in front of Budha, he was on his knee in front of that divine soul. Budha guided him to realise his inner soul and made him understand putting that branch back to its position is not an easy task. If you could not do this, you got no right to murder innocent people. After that incidence, Angulimal became a true followers of Budha. He used to accompany Budha in public, people threw stones at him to take revenge of their dear once. Angulimal was silently taking that hostile atmosphere as atonement of his sin that he had done in the past.

Valmiki Muni : In another story about the composer of *Ramayaa.* The Valmiki Muni was a notorious dacoit at one point of time. He used to loot people and that is how he used to run his livelihood and feed his family. One day, he met mythical "Naradji" the messenger of God. Narad asked him why are you doing all this? Valmiki said for my family. Narad asked to Valmiki that go and ask your family, will they be the responsible of your sin, though you are doing all this for them only. Valmiki went and asked the same question to his mother and father. They said we do not know from where and how you are earning this money and how you running our livelihood? It is very clear that we are not going to be the responsible of your wrong-doing. You, only you are responsible for this, we are not. Valmiki got his answer and had self-realisation and later on he has written the famous and the most popular epic The *Ramayana.* Now, you must have understood the God has not chosen that job for Valmiki. But he was doing something else. The God has chosen for him to write. If he wouldn't have met Naradji then he would have kept doing the same thing. Valmiki was the same person but after meeting Naradji. He transformed himself to become a different person after hearing his inner-soul.

Sachin Tendulkar : In today's scenario there are several references with whom we can take inspiration. Everybody is familiar with "Sachin Tendular's name. He heard his inner-soul much earlier. At the age of 15, he was representing India. Don't you think it is a miracle? He comes from a very common family background. Today you just name any record related to cricket world that he had not broken. He is just a twelveth standard student. He doesn't have much qualification but today he is the pride of the nation and for the entire world. Things happened automatically in his carrier, he just played cricket, nothing else. Today not only India but entire world is accepting that he is the God of cricket. How it is possible? Because, he has taken the job that God has chosen for him but he identified that much earlier in his life. If you asses his journey carefully his focus, concentration and God's blessing was always with him. Similarly, you should also identify your inner-being and concentrate on your work. There are some more examples that we would like to share with you.

Bhagat Singh : Shaheed Bhagat Singh was born on September 28, 1907. His father was also a revolutionary, so patriotism flowed in his blood. By the time, he completed his secondary education; Bhagat Singh knew everything about the revolutionaries of his family. At the- age of thirteen, Bhagat Singh left school and joined the freedom movement.

At that time, there was a powerful anti-foreign cloth movement in the country. Bhagat Singh took part in this movement and wore only *Khadi.* He realised in his young age what was suitable for him and what he should do. We all know he had rightfully been given the title of Shaheed-e-Azam the King of Martyrs.

Jerry Yang's father died when he was only two years old. Yang moved to San José at the age of ten years only with his mother and brother. He said that even if his mother was an English teacher, he knew only one word (shoe) on his arrival in the United States.

Yang is graduated from the Sierramont Middle School, and Piedmont Hills School and he received his BS and MS degrees in electrical engineering at Stanford University, where he was a member of Phi Kappa Psi fraternity.

In 1994, Jerry Yang founded Yahoo! with David Filo. Their aim was building the first directory of websites on Internet. Initially, this directory of websites called "Jerry's Guide to the World Wide Web".

They worked on this project during their studies at Stanford University. But quickly, the website got a big success following the development of the web. Yahoo! decided to popularise the concept of portal including content and services. In 2005, the company announces a turnover of $ 5.2 billion, a net income of $ 1.9 billion thanks to a workforce of 11,000 employees.

Henry Ford : Henry Ford a famous Automobile manufacturer. Henry Ford was born on July 30, 1863, on his family's farm in Dearborn, Michigan. From the time he was a young boy, Ford enjoyed tinkering with machines. Farm work and a job in a Detroit machine shop afforded him ample opportunities to experiment. He later worked as a part-time employee for the Westinghouse Engine

Company. By 1896, Ford had constructed his first horseless carriage which he sold in order to finance work on an improved model.

Ford incorporated the Ford Motor Company in 1903, proclaiming, "I will build a car for the great multitude." In October 1908, he did so, offering the Model T for $950. In the Model T's nineteen years of production, its price dipped as low as $280. Nearly at $15,500,000 were sold in the United States alone.

Mark Zuckerberg: Mark Zuckerberg was born on May 14, 1984 and grew up in the suburbs of New York, Dobbs Ferry. He was the second of four children and the only son in the educated family. Mark's father, Edward.

Zuckerberg, is a dentist and mother, Karen Zuckerberg, is a psychiatrist. His father used to do dental practice next to the family house. Mark and his three sisters, Arielle, Randi and Donna were raised in Dobbs Ferry, New York.

Mark got interested in programming yet in elementary school. The fact that the world is divided between programmers and users as Mark found out when he was 10 years old and got his first PC Quantex 486DX on the Intel 486.

From Mark Zuckerberg biography, we found out he was taught Atari BASIC Programming by his father and when Mark was about 12, he used Atari BASIC to create a messenger, which he called "ZuckNet". It made all the computers connected to each other and allowed to transfer messages between the house and dental office. His father installed the messenger on his computer in his dentist office and the receptionist could inform him when a new patient arrived. Mark also enjoyed developing games and communication tools and as he said he was doing it just for fun.

Jawed Karim : Jawed Karim was born in 1979 is a Bangladeshi-German internet entrepreneur. He is best known for being the co-founder of the popular video-sharing website YouTube. Many of the core components of PayPal, including its real-time anti-fraud system, were also designed and implemented by Karim.

While working at PayPal, he met Chad Hurley and Steve Chen. Then three years later he founded the YouTube video-sharing website in 2005. YouTube's first video, *Me at the Zoo*, was uploaded by Karim on April 23, 2005.

After co-founding the company and developing the YouTube concept and website with Chad Hurley and Steve Chen, Karim enrolled as a graduate student in computer science at Stanford University while acting as an advisor to YouTube. When YouTube was acquired by Google, Karim received 137,443 shares of stock, worth about $64 million based on Google's closing stock price at the time.

In March 2008, Karim has launched a venture fund called Yo University Ventures, with the goal of helping current and former university students to develop and launch their business ideas.

Baba Ramdev : There are so many examples of people, who heard their voice of soul and got immense success. Once Baba Ramdev, the famous *yoga* guru described about his success, said he was born in a very poor family somewhere in Alipur, Hariyana. When he was just 14 years old young boy, he decided to come to Haridwar. He came to Haridwar by a local bus and somehow he could manage his staying and education in Haridwar with the help of his various *Guru*. He could study *Vedas* in detail. Learnt *yoga* according to our ancient tradition and gradually introduced the power and strength of *yoga* to the entire world. When asked Swamiji, you have created such a big empire of your own, he told humbly that he has not done anything, it is God's wish. Whichever way God has guided him he moulded himself, nothing else. You must be thinking that how can someone become like Sachin Tendulkar and Baba Ramdev. Here we want to tell you with our firm-belief that they were also a common people at one point of time. We generally find people who come from a most common and ordinary background, later they become highly successful in their life.

Mr Malhotra : India-Pakistan 1947 partition tragedy made a deep scars to the psyche of the millions people of this country. Mr Malhotra was also one of the victims of this tragedy. He too migrated with his family from Pakistan. He left everything behind when he came to India with his family. They settled down in a refugee colony. The family faced new challenges to manage both ends meet like food, clothe, poverty and livelihood. He passed his childhood in abeject poverty and it was painful to him. He saw his mother used to work as a domestic help. He too has worked with his mother as a helper at the age of 13 years. As a child he used to see the difference between labour and the contractor. The contractor of the construction site used to come every day. He has seen him always sitting at the chair and doing nothing instead ordering labourer. As a child Mr Malhotra was inquisitive about this situation that why this man is the owner of this site? Why we are working as labourer? He decided that one-day he will also work as an owner. As a young man, he started his small business but couldn't get success. He created many companies one by one but he failed utterly and he was virtually on the road.

One of his executives working as an account head in Mr Malhotra's company. His name was Mr Balbhadra Agrawal who was carrying a legacy of business understanding and had exposure of working in Birla organisation. He had suggested him one-day that he can do product marketing better than anything else. He told Mr Malhotra that you have got interest and knack both in it. Why don't you go for it? He further suggested that many people cannot do this and it has got immense scope also. Taking this suggestion from his executive Mr Malhotra again started another company called "belle bra" that was dealing in bra-making business. He did not have money at all. He borrowed some money from his closed relative assuring him that when he will have money, he will pay back him with interest.

This time he used his product marketing skill and achieves a turnover of Rs 25 crore P.A. He becomes a millionaire. He is still surprised and shocked that how that miracle happened. Who did this after all. Today the turnover of his company is more than 250 million annually. He created a brand in bra history, named "teenager Bra". This is a story of a common man who identified his job that God has specifically chosen for him. He concentrated only on marketing part and "Teanager Bra" has become the unique in that category, being number-One in bra industry.

Survival of the Fittest

Today the general saying in "survival of the fittest" has become outdated. Time and conditions have changed. There are ample options are available, the mind-set of the people have changed. Opportunities are knocking at your door, if all these factors are easily accessible then why a person can't become a successful? Rather than blaming yourself all the time, one should sit calmly and think where is the fault?

In older time, there was a tradition of slavery. Do you think when men were living their life as a bonded-labour and all the development related opportunities were not possible? They did not have any idea what their future would be? What their life would be? The industrial revolution has changed the scenario of the entire world. The revolution produced leaders who supported common people to show their strength and leadership skills. The leaders have taken their responsibilities and there were leaders for development. If you will closely observed today's scenario, the mainstream people of the society not only supporting common people but they are also giving them leadership training to grow in life. Today, there is full of possibilities, it has got long historical background of technological developments and innovations. In a brief, if you cannot achieve your aim in this golden time then when will you do it?

It is very important that one should know his ability and potential. He should hear the voice of his or her inner-soul. He should start thinking in which area he can be useful to get success. If you will select the work according to your taste and you get the maximum result, as well as have peace and happiness? You will thank your God at least 10 times in a day. With this aptitude don't you think you will be contributing your bit to the society or in the development of the nation?

You have take the initiative but first of all you will have to understand your ability. You will have to identify your soul's direction and will have to work according to the instruction of your soul. By doing this, your life will be transformed completely and you will surprise the world that how things have changed automatically in your life. Whosoever has adopted this route of self-realisation, he has got real happiness, immense success and a healthy life to set a precedent for others, who can take a cue from you.

We often see people do hard work and tried every possible way to get success, even they do various rituals and practices. They keep on trying and adopt one or the other methods but do not get success in life despite putting all their efforts. Have you ever thought why they are not getting success? We will again focus on this, the God has chosen a specific work to do for them but they have still not could able to reach to get it. They are struggling to find that most suitable job that is waiting for them. We generally noticed that people say, they are not happy with their job but they continue and keep on doing for years the same job. They do not enjoy their work at all. They are forcing themselves to do it whereas their inner conscious does not allow them to do so.

Just think about that situation, how come a person become successful if he is not doing the work that is giving him satisfaction, enjoyment and happiness. There are thousands of examples, who heard his inner soul, identified it and worked according to the instruction of the soul has got definite success in life.

The great philosopher **Swami Vivekananda** described it beautifully:

Take up one idea. Make that one idea your life. Think of it, dream of it, live on that idea. Let the brain, muscles, nerves, every part of your body, be full of idea, and just leave every other idea alone. This is way to success.

The great philosopher Swami Vivekananda used to tell [illegible]

2

Who has not Heard the Soul

Hear Inner-Soul

You must be wondering why we are focussing again and again to hear your inner-soul to follow the instruction of your soul only. Here we want to discuss some incidents where in spite of constant reminder of soul, people ignored it and their life took a strange turn that they had not even imagined in their dreams. You must be aware about a latest incident in which a billionaire businessman was shot dead in his farm house. By profession, he was a property dealer. He started his carrier as a teacher, later on he realised that the teaching profession is not suitable for him and so he got into the property business. He got immense success in that business and created an empire by hook or crook. He was known to be the property business tycoon among his business circle.

It was a major news in the television and newspaper saying that "a billionaire businessman was murdered in Delhi". Television and newspaper were constantly giving his news and trying to find out the exact reason behind the murder. When media agencies investigated that news in detail they found that the businessman was having disputes in the family on property issue. He had two sons.

His wife was not staying with him. She was staying with his younger son. Elder son was staying alone with his family and Mr Businessman was staying in his farmhouse alone with another lady. They said businessman was so greedy that he was not allowing any of his family members, neither his wife nor his sons to become a part of his property, though both his sons were expecting a major chunk in his property. He was not ready to give them their dues. He used to humiliate them in front of everybody. He didn't behave as the head of the family. There were so many other things that led of his gruesome murder.

Last six months of his life were terrible. He was scared, terrified and appalled. He knew it that he will be murdered very soon. He got an intuition and he immediately increased his security. Now ten security guards were providing him protection all the time, day and night. The interesting thing in this story was that he was shot dead when he was absolutely alone. No one was with him for his security. The saddest part of this story is his own younger son designed the conspiracy of his murder.

Here is a point that one needs to understand. What is use of that money that he earned with great effort? What is the use of that huge empire that he had created for himself? In spite of having everything, he lived his life in hell and like a loner. He was physically alive, but do you think that he was actually alive? For the last six months, he was like a moving dead body. Imagine the amount of pressure, pain and suffering he must have gone through. Was he really living a life that he wanted to? What could be the worst than this that his own son did the conspiracy of his murder. He definitely must have done something wrong because he was the father of his son. Mr Businessman has ample time to inculcate the ethics and moral values in his son. The unfortunate part was he could not spare time for all this and was mistaken by the thought that money is everything. His inner-soul must have instructed him, warned him, raised objection several times but he could not hear his soul. We can say he completely ignored his soul and so see the result. Here we want to tell you that your soul will always guide you in a right direction. Mr Businessman lost that opportunity and one day he was murdered by his own progeny. It is not a murder only that one can think off. It was a murder of faith, murder of trust, murder of hope and a murder of beautiful relation in the world that father and son cherish together. Yes, it is a murder of humanity.

Here, we will have to understand this point in detail that why it happened? The point is, there is no integrity in people these days. Integrity means if something does not belong to you, it is not yours. You should not take it. Your right is to take anything that you have earned or achieved with good intension and you should feel proud of that. Today people with power and politics earn huge amount of money by hook or crook without realising that they are encroaching the right of somebody, who is vulnerable and he or she can not do anything. Do you think that "somebody" will spare you? He will curse you for your act and you will not get peace on this earth.

Not to Ignore Soul

This is the story of a greedy businessman. His soul must have warned many times but he continued, he ignored his inner-soul. He must know that he was doing wrong but continued for money and to get power. He definitely must have gone through a lot of pain and sufferings before his death. After his murder, the entire family got devastated. Now, son is in lock up. The unfortunate mother cannot do anything but just to accept the reality and live with this turmoil and disturbance. Just think for a moment, if he would have heard his soul, would the entire family see this tough time in the from of disgrace and shameful.

Apart from that painful incident of year 2013, I want to take this discussion further to another incident, so that it is be clear that everything is related to our soul. Soul is the most important element in our body. We can not ignore it at any cost and if you will ignore it then be ready to face the consequences.

It was very astonishing to read one morning in the newspaper that another businessman was shot dead by his real brother. The businessman was the tycoon of real state. Uncounted property sites, lands, housing projects, shopping malls and cinema halls belonged to him. In a short span of time, he had become the billionaire. It was the rag to riches story. I came to know through media agencies that it was a family dispute. The younger brother was demanding his property portion in the farmhouse where both the brothers were staying with their family. They were fighting over the farmhouse property. The elder brother was not ready to share with his younger brother and one day this filmy drama came to an end. Both the brothers had come in the afternoon for lunch. They had an argument over the disputed farmhouse. Younger brother took out gun and fired on his elder bother. He was dead then and there. In this filmy gun fire sequence the security guards of elder brother also fired at younger brother. Within few minutes both the brothers were quiet forever and the farmhouse is still there. Now, what is use of such a big empire? They had everything but they were fighting over a small farm house. If they would have invested this money for some good cause, would have heard their soul and not ignored it, would that situation occur?

Human being is the best creation of God on this earth. Almighty has created our body with five important elements, i.e., "Fire, Air, Water, Earth and Sky". God has created all our body parts patiently and unique way. He designed some of the important parts in our body like heart and brain. Our body works on their instructions.

We generally forget that the most important element existing in our body is "The Soul", and many of us are unaware of its power and strength. We will understand this in great detail but let's first talk about the best creation of God.

Everyday is a new day. Till morning to evening you do your daily routine work to run your livelihood. You take decisions while working, dealing, talking and meeting with different people. All those decisions are the result of your heart and brain. Sometimes you are satisfied with your decision, sometimes not. At times you are confused on your own decision. There is a situation when you are stuck in a dilemma and your brain does not work. We all are part of this and that's how people live their life. When you take any wrong decision, it affects you directly but indirectly it is affecting your close ones also like your family members. Also if your family members are taking any decision, you will be affected by their decisions. It is from both the sides and that is how we live life and try to achieve our aspirations and dreams.

Control Desire

Now, the question is who forces us to take those decisions in our daily normal life? According to The *Geeta*, Lord Krishna described *Inderiyan* as your desires that are related to your heart. You should control your heart means you should control your desires. Brain tries to control your desires. There is a popular portrayal in *Geeta* where Lord Krishna is delivering his knowledge *The Gyan* to Arjuna. In that picture, horses are representing your desires and the bridles are controlling these horses. These bridles are representing your brain that controls your desires.

Today's man is exposed to so many things in this materialistic world. We generally get attracted towards so many things in our daily life. We try to control our desires but often these desires overpower us and we become their slave. We indulge ourselves in some bad habits like drinking, smoking, prostitution and extra-marital affairs. After some time, we become vulnerable to the situation and it is difficult to get rid of them. Later on, we face the music of these consequences.

Here we want to share two hypothetical examples with you. Suppose there is a poor family residing in your locality. One day you see a local politician or a goon giving threats to the head of the poor family. The intention of the goon is to grab his house. He tries to compel him to sell his house forcefully. In spite of money temptation, the poor man does not agree for selling his house to him. The politician gives him life threat but he is not ready to listen because without that house where will he go? Where his family will stay?

The poor man is adamant and not ready to leave his house at any cost. The goon beats him up and throws his belonging on the road and asks the family members to leave the house instantaneously. Poor fellow lied down on the ground and began to entreat in front of him but it was of no use imploring in front of a criminal like him. Just think for a moment, is this the right way to deal with poor people? Don't you think, it is the misuse of power asking someone to vacate his own house like this?

The intention of the local politician was that after demolishing the house, at the same place he will construct some shops to increase his profit. He saw his profit but could not see his injustice would ruin a poor family. He dealt a heavy blow to the poor man with bad intention.

In another situation that local politician shares his vision with poor man that he wants to open an orphanage. He tries to convince him with good intention to open such centre; he tells him that his house will be the perfect location. He further convinced poor fellow that if he has any objection they can work together for this good cause. Local politician tells him clearly that he will not bargain with him and will pay a reasonable price of the house.

Also, the local politician will construct a new house for him in a good location. If there is a mutual understanding on that proposal, don't you think this is the right way to deal a poor man.

Action and Intention

Here, the intention is more important rather than action. There is a major difference between action and intention. In the first situation, intention of the local politician was bad, whereas in the second situation, his intention was good. If you observe minutely, in both the situations, action is same but intentions differ.

In a nutshell, if your intention is right it means your decision is right. If your intention is wrong, in that case your decision will also be wrong. There are several examples from our society that people who are criminals and act like a goons, suffer a lot in their life. They do not get mental peace and happiness and lead a physically sick life that is full of pain and sufferings. The families of such people also suffer a lot along with them because of their wrong attitude and bad intention.

We often see in our daily life that the money earned from dishonesty, deceitfulness, fraudulence and corruption will not be of any use. It cannot give you mental peace, happiness and enjoyable life. It is an irony that the money you are earning from various means for your family, will not give you any reward. Instead of you can see his wife, sons and sons- in-law are often seen murdering their father for that money.

Now, the question is why a man gets indulging in such wrong practices? For whom he wants to accumulate so much of money? Why has he become more and more greedy with time? Many of us are well aware about the repercussions of these situations but we do not have control on our desires. These desires are so powerful that we want to fulfill them at any cost. We generally adopt various wrong means to earn money. It has become a fashion in the society that everybody wants to live with a fat bank balance. They all live with this wrong notion that money is the real success and it will give them peace and happiness. It has been noticed that the people who earned money from various wrong means, mostly suffer from severe diseases like cancer, sugar, heart-attack, and insomnia in their life. Neither they can eat properly nor can have a sound sleep. They cannot live a healthy and normal life.

Either they are worried about money or death. They live an unsatisfied and fearful life. They die with their unsatisfied desires. When a person dies with his unsatisfied desire, his bad *karmic* account is carried forward in his next life. The *karmic* account means, whatever good or bad you do in your present life, it is your account. It means, when a person will take rebirth he will have to clear his account of his previous life as well as the last account. That's how this human life-cycle revolves. People take birth, die and in their next birth they have to clear their balance account. This is the life-cycle of uncounted birth of human being. According to the Hindu mythology, if you clear all your account you will get *moksha*. It means you are free from this prison of life. You need not to come again on this earth. You will be promoted to next stage of improved life.

Let's take an example to understand this in detail. Suppose a ninth class student has failed in his class, now how can you expect him to study in 10th class, until he is qualified to the next class? He will not be able to study in 10th class. He will be again studying in 9th until he passes that class with grade. The same is with human being. We are failing again and again that is why we are taking rebirth again and again on this earth. Whatever, we are doing good or bad in this present life, it is due to our past *karmas*. We are providing material to God to create ourselves. The material that we are providing to God is jealousy, lust, greed, distrust and cheating along with many unsatisfied and untold desires.

It is natural that whatever you give to others, they will also return the same. If you give them thorns and stones, you cannot expect to get beautiful flowers from them. In the same manner, you can't expect that you give God, jealousy, lust, greed, distrust and cheating and then expect a good life from him. He is not a fool. After all, he is the creator of this entire universe. You cannot fool around with him. He does not have anything to give you. Whatever you provide him he will pay it back. Now, the choice is yours.

Materialistic Life

This materialistic life is like a prison. Every human being is bound to live with it. We have to clear our accounts in this life. We often read in the newspaper, a prisoner from X jail ran away by breaking the locker of the prison. Police finds him and this time he gets more punishment. We are also living in a jail, where we have to clear our account of our last and this life also. That is why we are born but people commit suicide and do not want to pay back their account. They destroy their physical body. They take birth again and get double punishment like real prisoners.

That is why, a man should clear his old account and in this life he should hear the voice of his soul and control his life according to this divine voice. Your knowledge and wisdom along with your *karmic* accounts also gets carry forward in new life. With the consent of heart, brain, soul and the knowledge that you have got from your last birth, you should find a suitable job for yourself. By doing so, you will achieve immense success and spirituality. This will happen only when you correct your input rather than blaming someone. It is a notable fact that your input is in your control. You have got no control over output. You can't correct people and it is not your job also but yes, you can correct yourself, and correct your input to live with peace. But it is very difficult for people to accept their own mistakes. They blame people till their last breath.

If you understand yourself, correct yourself, you can peep deep down that whatever you are doing at the moment is with your soul's consent, believe me you are on the right path.

Mukti or Moksha

If you are not on the right path you will not get *Mukti.* This means you will not be free from this prison of life. We will discuss about *"Mukti or Moksha"* later, but now I will try to tell you that, why Mahatma Budha, Lord Mahaveera and Gurunanak have not taken rebirth on this earth again. Actually, they cleared all their accounts and became divine souls. They lived a peaceful, enjoyable life and showed the right path to misguided ones. They have showed the human being - *Mukti Duwar.* They all got passed with grade in their life and were never born again. Now, it is their wish to take birth on this earth to show a light to every human being. That is why we find a couplet in holy *Geeta:*

Yada yada hi dharmasya, glanir bhavati bharata,
abhyutthanam adharmasya, tadatmanam srjamy aham,
praritranaya sadhunam, vinashaya cha dushkritam,
dharamasansthapnaya, sambhavami yuge-yuge.

Means,

"Whenever and wherever there is a decline in religious practice, 'O descendant of *Bharata*', and a pre-dominant rise of irreligion—at that time I descend myself, for the protection of the good, for the destruction of the wicked and for the establishment of righteousness, I am born in every age."

Otherwise these divine souls will live in peace wherever they are.

Sometimes people do good and bad. They will have to come on this earth for their wrong-doings. They will have to come to pay their account because they had no connection with their soul. They were not aware of the power of their soul.

After giving such a detailed background, now we will talk about the soul. If a person identifies his soul, develop a connection with it and hears his inner-voice then how he can achieve true happiness in life? How he can be free from this world?

Divine Power

First of all, we will have to understand in detail what the soul is? According to us there is one universal power or a divine power exists in this universe that is controlling this inner and outer world. We are also part of that super power. You may call this super power "God". According to Hindu mythology, he is everywhere. Soul is the important element of God in our body. It is our inner-being, the super power, the universal strength, the infinite power, the living element that is giving us instruction, signs, it raises objection and it warns. It is the cycle of breath that constantly running from your birth. Your breath or *Pranwayu* is always in action, even if your body taking rest, sleeping, dreaming, walking and eating but breath never stops. Don't you think, these breaths are the only factor in your body that is gives a feeling that you are alive? Without breaths your body is like a dead body. The day this cycle breaks, the value of this body is nothing. After the death your close ones make hurry for your cremation. What is important then your body or soul? It means the element of God or divine power that exists in you is valuable, eternal, pure and divine. It is dynamic, mature, indifferent and detached in its nature. It is away from greed, attachment, jealousy and distrust. Who identifies that divine power within only he can connect to the God and achieve that divine element in him.

Now, we will try to understand this point in this materialistic world. For instance, you are the owner of one company and there are more than hundred people are working under you. People are working on various posts, some are on upper post and some are on lower post. We often see there is trend that owner of the company keeps scolding his employees. You talk less to his employees. You never talk to his employees with smile. You never eat and sit with them. You think that you are "The Owner" of this company and you should not do all this. This is the kind of nature and behaviour that you adopt with your employees. What will you say is it fine? If you will go by today's trend, logically you will prove this absolutely right. You are free to think like that but to avoid the system of God is beyond the control of any human being.

If we are talking about the God, then every human being whosoever is taking birth on this earth is reborn with the element of God. We will not see inequality in nature. God treats every person equal. Now the interesting thing is the company owner is a soul and the peon who is working for you is also a soul. Both of them are giving their contribution as par their specified role. Because of his *karma* in last berth and this life, the peon is working on the lower post. If we talk about the boss, you are also paying your account in this life as an important worker for your own company. Both of them have chosen their work according to their knowledge and physical capacity. Now, it is destiny that one is working as boss and other serving his bit as peon. But the element of God "The Soul" is equal in them. The general tendency is the boss is supposed to be the big person and the peon who is working under him should be treated like a small man. But in reality both of them have born on this earth as a failed student and paying their accounts. Now, who takes birth where? It is the result of their *karma*.

You generally help someone and it is also true that you take help from others. Often people have misunderstanding that they helped someone, they go and paint the city red that just because of them the other fellow is alive, they changed his life. People claim that because of their great efforts, many schools are running, children are getting education in many schools that are run by them, many orphanage centers have been opened. They think that they are the God on this earth and they should be treated like a God in his locality or in their surroundings. After some time, we see them participating in local politics. Their intention was something else. Now, the point is why a man thinks that he is the survivor? Why he tries to behave like a God? If these arrogant and hippocratic people could do welfare of the humanity then what is the need of God?

Actually, the people, whose thinking is like that, cannot be useful to the society. They are nobody to claim that because of their effort welfare of the people is happening. The point is whatever we do in our daily life, be it interaction with people or business dealing etc. Actually, we do not deal with people directly. It is dealing with the God. We just become the medium in between the God and that fellow. We only become the reason for good cause. The God will not select people for just like that if he will chose someone to serve humanity, country, community and society. Almighty will see the ability of the person whether he or she is able and suitable or not. With good intention, honesty and soft behaviour you become the chosen one by the God. And that is the result of your devotion and dedication. That is why the almighty selects you to do something for some good cause. He selects you among millions of people to execute that particular task that will serve the humanity.

This is the finner point generally people missed and think that they are only capable or able people on this earth to do good work. They forget about the God. You think that he is one who is doing everything. You frequently tell people because of his hard work you became rich not because of God's blessing. God gives you a chance to do something but you involved in luxurious life and start satisfying your unwanted desires.

God's Blessings

You must have seen normal people in your locality, suddenly you come to know that fellow has multiplied his business like anything, within a short span of time you see his total transformation. If the God select someone do to a good job, he gives him lot of money to do. We notice, earlier that fellow used to be very humble, decent, well-mannered and God-fearing, the sudden change in his life adds so many things in his behaviour like arrogance, way of talking to the people, life-style that depends on show off. He indulges in bad practices. His soul warns him, but he ignores and become the slave of powerful desires and totally engrossed from top to bottom.

We need to understand clearly, when God selects someone for good cause, it means he is an able person and he should do that work with full dedication and forget about its result and expectation. He is just a medium and will become the means for some good cause. If you are successful, it is a sign that God has blessed you to do some good work.

There is a decision of your soul apart from heart and brain. We often ignore our voice of soul and give priority to heart and brain and often face the consequences. The soul is the powerful tool in our body. It is the element of

God in you. Ignoring it, means we go against the will of God. From this point, the fight starts among body, heart, brain and soul. At the end, a man accepts the truth of reality and kneels down in front of God.

Let's talk about if a man would hear his soul before commencing the work or during and after the work, he will not only get a peace and happiness in his life but the entire society will also be benefitted. You must be shocked to hear that how it is possible?

First of all, if the person will do so, it may take time but he will get sure success. Hearing your soul means you are following the path that has got God's consent. Be sure that you cannot be wrong. To know the right path, selecting it and to follow that with full dedication and confidence without any disturbance is a major task that shows your successful personality. When you identify your right path there will be many challenges that you will have to face. And you have to be ready for that. At times, you feel disturbed, confused and will not be able to decide whether you should go in that direction or take some different route. In such a situation, your close ones like friends, wife, mother and father become your guide. They may be having their own thoughts and beliefs. If you will start listening to all of them, it is confirmed that you will be in dilemma and will not be able to decide what to do.

Now let's think about it, why is that so? Whatever thought process they may be having those thoughts and beliefs are the result of their cultural values and the atmosphere in which they have been born and brought up and still living in that atmosphere. They will be giving their point of view which they think is right according to them. It is not necessary that it should be right according to your situation, because your education, surrounding situations, thoughts and beliefs will always differ from them.

Create Own Path

It is very interesting to know that though we live in this earth together but everyone is having his own question paper that he or she has to solve personally. Is it not shocking? Yes, God has made question paper for everyone, means each individual should answer that question paper. If your question paper of life is different than answer cannot be the same. But we mostly do that only, to solve our question we take the help of others, we follow them, want to give their answers like other solving. Just think about it how it is possible if each individuals question is different. Then why we follow people. This is your life you have to solve your own question paper separately. Nobody will come to solve your question paper. That is why, without distracting yourself and with the consent of your soul you should take important decision, and should select right path in life.

There will be a time while taking decision you will think about your family and children and will not feel confident. You will be in confused state of mind whether you should opt for it or not? One thing is clear, the decision that you will take inspired by your soul, will be a difficult path because it will be based on honesty and integrity. It will definitely lead you to towards real and permanent success in life. The path of success will always be full of challenges. If you will not accept the challenges, do you think you will be able to achieve high success in life? If you will be afraid with challenges and will take short cut in life. You will never be a successful in your whole life. A person who follow the direction of his own soul and work accordingly, his confidence will be thousand times more and he will not wait for anybody's help. He will do it himself and whatever he wants to say will say that with full confidence and in nonchalant manner. He starts treating every human being equally. He does not follow the route of people rather create his own path to get high success in life. He will be seen in the crowd separately. In his initial phase, people may ridicule or oppose him but when he becomes successful; people accept him and respect him. The 'father of the nation' beautifully describes:

First they ignore you, then they laugh at you, then they fight you, then you win.

—M.K. Gandhi

Life of such people becomes inspiration for others. Success automatically comes after. He gets money and respect more than enough that he has not dreamt in this life. He leads a blissful life. You may get such types of millions of examples in your own society, country and around the world. Now, the question is why it happened?

Again we are on that initial point, to hear your soul, one who hears his soul, follow its instructions. He only will be the beneficiary of the situation rest will only keep fighting in life. If you will start repeating success.....success every day, that way success will not come to you. Now, the point is if the soul has got such an important role in our life then why we ignore it? Let's discuss this also.

Whatever works you have chosen according to your taste, ability and with the consent of your soul, in that process you have to adopt several other things also. That will come as a package deal. You can not be in the position that "you want to have cake and eat it too". It is you are adopt or following the path of your soul then all the goodness should reflect in your behaviour honestly. For example, you should be honest and trustworthy, you will not hurt anybody, you will not tell a lie, you will keep yourself away from non-vegetarian food and you will not indulge in toxic sex related activities. In a nutshell, you have to keep yourself away from every bad habit that can distract you from your path. Now, the question is, are we ready for all this?

Today people are exposed to so many things. Things are at your doorsteps, things are easily available. Whatever you desire that will be available within few hours, be it liquor, non-vegetarian food and girls for entertainment. It is difficult for a person to keep away from them. But there is no dearth of such people who are on the right track. They are highly successful in life. The path of soul is difficult but it does not mean that one cannot do this. If the person is having full conviction and dedication then he should start working on his bad habits first. He should leave all his bad habits one by one. But the problem is nobody wants to follow this and yet they want success in life. Today everybody wants to be successful by hook and crook and think that the miracle of success will also happen in their life.

The day you start hearing your soul, you will be in a heavenly mode. This is beginning of yours to become a good person in life. You have to do one thing and you will see there will be long list of good things around you like, purity in food, purity of thoughts, honesty in relationship and truthful behaviour will automatically reflect in your personality.

Consent of Soul

I will make you understand this point by giving one interesting example. We all know the great scientist of the world Thomas Alva Edison invented electricity. Today the entire humanity is thankful to that great soul. Now, you see electricity is one thing but there are so many things that is related to electricity like fan, cooler, air-conditioner, freez, motor, washing machine, computer, internet etc, the list is long that all are useful to us. But without electricity, these all the electronic gadgets are of no use. Likewise, the soul is one but when you adopt is, start knowing it, identify it then our brain, heart and every part of our body will function properly and efficiently. If these body parts perform with the consent of soul, believe me they have got immense power to invent new inventions. New discoveries can be done easily.

Just think about that if a person selects his job after hearing his soul. His life takes a divine route that gives him mental peace, the peace and happiness in his family. He becomes the inspiration for family members. Children feel proud of his father. People around you also learn and inspire from your behaviour. The company of drinkers will be demoralised to that extent that man will get addicted to visit liquor shop daily and ruined himself completely. It is possibility that his drunkard friend will take some lesson from his life and start changing himself. His family will also get benefit from his changed behaviour. The money will be used properly and he will have that feeling that he is having less money. He will definitely contribute something to the humanity, for his society and country. The next generation will respect him and will give example of his achievements. He will be in a position to gather huge amount.

Every individual has some qualities in ability and strength, but all this is possible only through the process of soul enlightenment. You have example of dacoit Angulimal and Valmiki. The souls were already exiting in them but in spite of that they were indulging in those anti-social activities. But the moment their souls get enlightened, the whole world could see the change in their attitude. People actually do not know about the strength and the power of soul.

3

Why we did not Try to Know about Our Soul

Spiritual Knowledge

Now, you must have understood the strength of your soul. We want to tell you that only spiritual knowledge can purify you the most than any other knowledge. We want to stress that if a person hears his soul and work accordingly, nothing can challenge this blissful experience. Your selected work will become simpler, easier and enjoyable. On the other hand, if a person ignores his soul and selects his work according to his mind-set that this particular business or work will give him more money. Whereas he knows from inside that the work he has chosen is not correct and according to his taste and ability. Top of that he does not want to learn any new skill to work. When he will start doing that chosen work he will have to go through many difficulties and will face lot of complications. To do that work he will start playing tricks and become different. He will make fool of people, will adopt different types of ways and means to run that business anyhow. Have you ever thought why it happens? Because, the work you have preferred is not according to your taste and ability. You will keep doing that work life-long and can never get your desired goals. Finally, you will have to give up and will follow the ways and work system that already exists in the society. You can not add an extraordinary approach in your work, a different approach from the system that is adopted by others. You will also be the part of crowd. Mind you, it will be the main and the only reason why you can not achieve extraordinary success and peace in your life.

In another situation, if you do your work after hearing your soul then you will not require any type of extra effort. You will have to only follow the order of God with truth and honesty. You will not have any problem in your business. Your life will be easier and smooth. Then you need not to bluff people, torture, deceive and abuse anyone to get your work done. You will have clear-cut objective and you will set your destination in a playful manner. You will feel light within yourself and get eternal peace and happiness. Once *Swami* Ramdev said:

I have just followed the path of God, nothing else. The almighty guided me and I did the same without thinking about the outcome.

Everyone knows *Swami* Ramdev is a well-known personality of this nation. He is considered to be an international *Yoga Guru,* who enlightened millions of people, the huge benefits with his ancient *yoga* knowledge. In a brief, with the consent of soul one can do great work for the humanity. But the biggest irony is we never tried to identify our soul, we ignored its voice again and again though it warns you. Let's discuss in detail, why we did that? If you will scan your passed years of life for a moment, you will find that your soul warned you several times, given its indications but you ignored. You did not follow your inner-voice and faced the consequences.

The fast pace of metropolitan city has become the integral part of today's human being. You keep modifying your way of working according to the current trends. You copy other people and do your work. In fact, you can not use your creativity independently. You are more concerned about the society. You make the parameters of success by observing people, no matter how they are earning from various sources to become successful. You closely observe in the society that people respect such street- smart people who are earning money through all wrong means and create a respectable image in their society. They set an example in the society and people want to follow them.

Avoid Wrong-doing

As you know soul never gives its consent for any wrong-doing. It warns you again and again and indicates people that it is wrong, not right. But people think that it is the system of the society, and you must follow it up. You should not only follow that system but also try to prove that it is the right way in today's world. We often see when people did something wrong. They regret their decisions. They know within that they have done something wrong though they predict that they are happy. But the truth is they do not get mental peace anywhere. They go to the astrologers, numerologist, temples, and mosques and start believing in 'black magic' because of their dual personality. There are many painful instances have come to our notice that due to 'black magic' and superstitions they sacrifice innocent kids, hoping to have their own kid. You may say it is the strong influence of superstitions and 'black magicians' which worked on them. Such people go temple to temple, visit mosques, Gurudwaras, and Durgah to accept their sin. You often see such people in many crowded religious places. You can observe their faces and can easily make out, how frightened they are from inside and all the time praying to God that for getting help. Why it is happening because they are not getting peace anywhere. Their soul is constantly reminds them they have done something wrong earlier.

One thing is very clear, if you see the crowd in such places, it means, there is nothing for an intelligent people, the people who know the essence of the life. Have you ever seen crowd on the peak of the mountain, no, because rarely people reach on top. Crowd is just like a herd of sheep. It goes in one direction, where everybody is going without thinking. They are following that crowd blindly. People should look into their hearts and ask themselves that why they are blindly following that crowd which is not leading anywhere? They should understand the reality and accept their bad actions and should try to improve them. This is very important for the peacefulness of their body and soul. It might be possible that it feels difficult in the beginning but this effort will take you into another world. It is sure if you walk on this unbeaten path you will be successful and will get absolute internal peace and happiness.

You are like a student in the school of life. You will have to learn yourself rather than follow others with closed eyes. You know that generally people are not students and they don't have to learn anything. They think that they know everything. Correcting others is not our job. Our job is to correct ourselves first. You are the student and you will have to take your own responsibility. You can not get anything by following others who don't want to achieve anything in life. Its like to get into the next class you pass the examination. You have to clear your exams in this life. This means that you have to control yourself, like control on anger, jealousy and not getting involved the rat-race of life. Even if you win in that rat-race you will be a rat. You and only you need the awareness of soul that you are not a rat.

Karmic Account

Ignoring the voice of soul means, you are ignoring the voice of success, peace of mind, happiness and ultimately to almighty God. Generally, a person can not understand the essence of life, till he dies. He goes from this world dissatisfied. Then to complete his *karmic* account he keeps taking birth and rebirth again and again. But a person, who listens to his soul's voice, finds his goal in life and makes it meaningful. He shapes up his life and achieves high success. His life is filled with eternal peace and happiness. Money, respect and fame all walk into his life on its own. People who come in contact with these kinds of people also get affected positively and their influences help in making the society a better place.

Factors which are responsible for not hearing our soul also include our environment. Today, we have immersed ourselves so much in show-off and conceited that we can not see anything else. We try and project a false image all the time. Actually, in real life people have got different images which they keep flaunting in front of others. We spend on branded clothes. We lead an expensive life style. We spend more than our capacity in our marriages and so many other things. It is not necessary to spend this much, but we still spend more than our capacity. People do this for show-off in the society and satisfy their egos. To fulfill these unwanted desires and show-off people also take bribes from various ways to earn more money. They give expensive cars in marriages. Sometimes they take loans and even sell their property to plan a high-level marriage. By spending lavishly on marriage and food they think that a sacred ceremony like marriage needs alcohol, non-vegetarian and toxic foods to give it religious like flavour? We are settting a wrong precedent for our children by doing all this. We are not accepting the truth rather opting to display our wealth in shape of different forms like car, flat, branded garments. What is the use of show-off and bragging? We do not think for a second that what is the use of it? Why we are doing it? For whom we are doing it? Is there any requirement for that? People create their problems for themselves and try to justify that this is today's trend or demand. When they caught up in that restless and uneasy situation, they do not know how to come out? Then they don't get mental peace. They do not feel motivated and look older than their actual age. There is no fun in their life and they stop enjoying their life due to their worries and they have invited by adopting today's trend of the society.

Show-off and Bragging

Spending beyond your capacity, earning big money in order to getting name and fame in the society, show-off and bragging about your wealth and access to higher-ups lead you to a big problem in the life. People are not thinking on these points and practicing all these bad habits in the hope of getting more. Surely, it will not help anyone rather make your life burdensome and hell.

You might have seen people posing in such a way that they are the happiest person on the earth. In front of others, they pretend that they are very happy and they do not have any problem in their life. But with-in they are under the pit of deep problems due to jealousy, greed, frustration and disappointment. They show their money power even if they are earning that money through unethical means. You must have heard saying people, "he has his under the table income (or *do numbaree* income) also in the form of lakhs apart from his salary". What are we trying to say here? What kind of parameter we are setting in the society? We do not talk about the character of the man and his high moral values. We do not talk about his achievements. We do not consider our health and pure life as a gift of God rather busy in showing our money, gold, diamond and top of that we are trying to justify that bribing is ethical to give false image. People are living in the society with duplicity. One can clearly feel that people try to show that they are normal but within them, there is storm, a kind of restlessness and that reflects in their behaviour also. One can feel easily while talking to them. Is they are in their usual state of mind? Can you get mental peace in such a situation? That is why you will find mostly people are sick and caught-up in various illnesses. Once a well-known Hindi poet Ashok Chakradhar said:

Aaj wahi aadami sukhi hai jiska padosi dukhi hai, means

"A man is happy and well-settled, whose neighbour is in trouble"

Fictitious Life

People are fed-up by leading a bogus and fictitious life but they are not ready to change themselves due to societal norms. They are not ready to change their behaviour. They think whatever they are doing is right and people should follow them. Now, they do not know the difference between the good and bad. This is the result of their environment. The children also learn from your environment that you create for yourself. You knowingly or unknowingly learn so many things from your environment that are not right for our children and family. You know it from your heart that it is not right at all but you do not take 'U' turn and change your environment. You keep following that same path. Taking a 'U' turn means doesn't mean that you are a failure. It means you should accept your mistake, to change your way of working so that you can get a high success in life. To achieve that you need to do the commitment with yourself. Nobody will come to help you. You will have to change yourself forever.

Why we are saying this? Please try to understand with this example. When a child is born, does he carries with all the bad behaviours and habits that exist in our society like, theft, loot, jealousy, greed, lie, dishonesty and deceit? Obviously, the answers will be 'no. You will find that first you take birth on this earth then learn all the bad habits and behaviours one by one from your existing environment. Your environment is your biggest school and it plays an important role in your life. You need to separate yourself from your present environment and think. You need to adopt the way of self-study means book reading and find out the alternative of 'U' turn. Self-study will give you an insight that will lead you on a right direction. You will have to watch such spiritual channels that will give a vision about the life. By doing all this, you will be able to improve yourself as a better citizen of the society. Try to study and understand the life and culture of pure and successful people. This improvement only you can do it.

A real path that is always based on truth and honesty and that was followed by many successful people and they reached on top. You will also have to take honest route to get real and high success in life and that is not possible at all without hearing your voice of soul and consent. You may find it bit strange because there is possibility that it could be different from your education, nature and financial background. You can take a bold step in right direction only by getting knowing about all these factors. You will have to think where you want to move your life? You need to know which is the best way to get a good result?

You are the best creation of God and different from other human being. You are special among 7000 million people of this world. It is necessary that you need to know yourself completely. The God has not created you feeble but you present yourself cheap in this world. Have you ever thought about it? Why you do that? The main reason is, you can not recognise your unique ability, knack and capacity. There are loads of examples of people, who have not registered their presence as a rich people. They have recognised with their unique contribution. They have achieved high success in life according to their ability. It is the proven fact that money and power alaways create dishonest people. Money and power push you towards many unwanted desires. It doesn't mean that you should not earn money. You should earn money and live a peaceful and prospersous life but at the same time contribute your bit to humanity also by adopting right path.

Dusth-atma and *Divya-atma*

You must have heard people saying that he is a *Pret-atma*. He is *Dusth-atma* and that fellow is *Divya-atma*. It is the outcome of your environment. It gives the different names and identities like that. A man who is indulged in bad and malicious practices will be known as *Dusht-atma*. On the other hand, if a person is gentle and pure from his heart and always involved in the great service to the humanity is known to be *Divya-atma* or a divine soul.

You will get such examples in the society and in history. If you will try to find out the route cause of *Dusth-atma*, you will find it will surely in the society. These are the product of our society, our environment. If you will not correct your thoughts and make it favourable and healthy to grasp good behaviour and character till then you will not be able to hear your voice of soul. In today's confusion and chaos, it is possible that you will ignore your soul's voice again and again and will bound to suffer in life. You have to be strong enough to have a control on your desires than only you will be able to achieve the essence of life and higher success.

Let's find the answer of this question why you do not desire to know about your soul? When you clearly know your life can be filled with peace and happiness with soul. You can lead a meaningful life. You have to follow your soul and select specific work to do for yourself. You need not require any extra effort for that and you will not find any difficulty to do that if you hear your soul.

The main reason is your thinking has become polluted by unwanted desires. Our heart and brain overpower us and we do not have the single moment to know our soul. Most of the time you are thinking about your desires only and you want to fulfill them at any cost and anyhow. The biggest problem is today that you want to achieve everything in short span of time. There is saying in Sanskrit *Santosh Param Sukham* means 'contentment is happiness'. Today you will find nobody is contented. They do not have patience for things. They want everything but not with the honest way, they want to achieve that by hook and crook and at any cost. In such an environment, one can imagine that how a person can listen to his soul? There should be a strong desire within you to know your soul and keep your soul pure. Then only you can achieve positive results and find right path in life.

Santosh Param Sukham

It has become a general tendency of people that you do not want to know your soul and in this fast paced materialistic world. Having lots of money and all luxurious things can not guarantee you the real peace and happiness. You know it but you can not free yourself from the clutches of outer world. You should follow the way of soul which is full of divinity and purity. Nobody can stop you by doing this but most of the time you bother about those who are misguided, confused and do not have clarity where they are heading in their life. They are just the part of the crowd. You will not get anything by following such people. Do you think such type of people can help someone like you who are weak and not confidant? Now the point is why you get into such things when you know nothing will happen by doing all this. Many a times, people blame society. They say if this is the trend of the society then we have to follow it because we are part of this society. They try to justify their point with various arguments. According to him this trends is very much prevalent in society and because of societal pressure they had to follow them.

Now, the point is you are following things because society is doing it. But somewhere deep in your heart you know it very well that this is not right. But you are doing it without the consent of your soul. It means you are going against your soul's instruction and you are not blessed by God because you are ignoring your voice of soul. You should always remember that soul is the element of God. Can anyone get peace and happiness without God? Can you get high success in life without that supreme power? It is very simple, if you follow others and work accordingly, in that case the result will be the same. Nothing will change. You will get the average result. Actually, no one wants painful, disappointed and frustrated life but to follow others blindly can not give you a respectable and meaningful life. By doing all this you are not respecting yourself. If you will not respect yourself and raise your level, then how can you expect from your family and close one to respect you? You will have to make yourself useful to your family and society.

You must be wondering that how do I know my soul if it is that so important. We will surely help you out to identify your soul. You need not to do anything different. Initially, for knowing your soul, one day you need to work according to your soul, if you find it difficult then at least follow half-day this practice with patience. If you get peace, happiness, feel light after this practice and you get sound sleep then follow this practice for a week continuously and gradually increase one week to 15 days and then month and so on. It will become the part of your routine work. Believe us your life will be improved forever.

Positive Attitude

To get a high success in life, one needs to find out the people who are really successful and who are physically and mentally healthy and satisfied. He should take inspiration and seek guidance from them instead feeling jealous about their success and achievements. Generally, you neither want to interact with them nor want to know about them at all. It is well-known fact that if a person is successful, he must be having some values and principles in life. He is successful because he is different from others. There is always positive vibration around successful people. Whatever they do, they do it in an innovative manner. They behave decently and do not make other people short because they are not successful. They inspire them and help them to grow in life. They are very sensitive in their approach while interacting with people because they understand the feeling of other person. They have also gone through phases of life where they have seen many ups and downs. They understand each and everything because they have risen from the bottom and reached on top.

On the other hand, it has been noticed several time a mean person will make you feel as if you can not do anything in your life. You are good for nothing. He will degrade and disappoint you so much that you will not have courage to stand up in life of your own. We strongly think that you should give due importance to those people who are successful in life. They are achievers and leading a respectable life with pride. You should get inspiration from them without getting into that which cast, community and religion they belongs to. You need to observe and study what are made them successful.

You watch films. Do you know why hero always gets success? Why he is the winner at the end? The character of hero is always based on some moral values and principles.

Though your soul gives instructions that you go and meet that successful man but your jealous behaviour stops you. You are not ready to do any kind of improvement in your life. You keep moving in your same environment and do not want to come out. Finally, you accept that same environment and one day your life ends with that jealousy and greed. Now, you have chosen such life then whom you will blame? It is entirely up to you what you want to do. Everything is inside you. Everything is in your soul. It is pure element in body. It may covered with dust for some time by it is hundred per cent pure. It is your duty to keep it clean and pure.

It has been noticed that you do not have control on your outer world. You have got no control on output of the people. They are bound to give their output. You should not worry about that. You need to correct your input that is in your control. No matter what people are saying or giving it to you but you should correct your input. You should accept yourself as it is and start loving yourself. You need to respect yourself. Things will start taking shape in right direction automatically. There will be new thoughts and beliefs emerge in your mind. These will be according to your nature and behaviour that are specifically designed by God for you. To clarify such thought we are taking these quotes:

Where can we go to find God if we can not see him in our own hearts and in every living being.

—Swami Vivekananda

A man is but the product of his thoughts what he thinks, he becomes.

—M.K. Gandhi

Be sure you put your feet in the right place, then stand firm.

-Abrahim Lincon

You can't cross the sea merely by standing and starting at the water.

-Rabindra Nath Tagore.

To get a high success in life one has to hear his inner-voice, the soul. It flashed again and again, warned you several time but you ignored. To get a hint of your soul is entirely up to you. It is natural and will keep happen in your life but when you will response to voice of your soul is up to you. Whosoever has heard the voice of his soul got immense success and peace in life. The great scientist of the world Thomas Alva Edison saw lightening in the sky and discovered electricity that served the humanity as whole. All the great people, who have took berth on this earth were highly sensitive and worked according to their soul. They thought for the humanity and have not shifted their vision or thought for tomorrow. They immediately got involved in their project and took action with full conviction and confidence. It is solely up to you what you want to be in your life.

In every era, there was bad and good people always. You can take the example of Lord Rama and Ravana, Lord Krishna and Kansh–people were there in every era and they exist in today's world also. All kinds of people are there doing various kinds of businesses. It depends on you what you want to become and not on the society. World is the same, society is the same, you have to learn and improve your life. For this you will have to understand this example. When you put a tap in the ground, it gives dirty water initially. After some time, you see less dirty water and after some more time, its starts giving clean water. Our system is also like this. Whatever dirt we have inside we have to clean that. First dirt will come out and when you keep cleaning yourself you will find your soul is getting purified. Whenever you start a fresh, it is always a new beginning. Nothing is lost even now we still have time. Everybody needs to introspect. We need to look into our past and try to know when our soul tried to say something to us. Then think why we did not listen to our soul? These are few questions that one needs to find out.

Without getting there answers, you will not be able to develop a relationship with your soul.

Introspection

To know your soul you need to know yourself first. Introspection can give you knowledge, what you have to do and what don't have to do? You will have to ask yourself very honestly that how many times your soul tried to give you a new massage. You might have done that work for few days then you ignored it that was the massage from God and from your soul. You didn't give any importance to it. For instance, suppose a white shirt has a spot you also know that, this spot is not permanent. That spot can be removed but you will have to clean it. It is possible that the spot does not go in one wash. It is also possible that the spot does not go in three to four washes, but it is not possible that it doesn't go even in 20 washes. If you have the strong desire to follow God's command, then you will be able to follow it. When you sow a seed, it also doesn't grow up into a tree in one day. So one should listen to his soul's voice, make a promise and follow God's decisions. Rest of the way God will show you himself. There are many examples in this world, where people have attained success at any age. For example Prabhupadji, who laid the foundation of Eskon temple at the age of 74 and propagated Hare Rama, Hare Krishna all over the world. Apart from him there will be many other examples of people, who got success in their later stages of life.

Here we want to discuss some more successful people, who achieve success in their later life.

Anna Mary Robertson Moses : Anna Mary Robertson Moses who was known as Grandma Moses also was a renowned American folk artist. Grandma Moses first came to public attention in 1940, at the age of 80. She began painting in her seventies after abandoning a career in embroidery because of arthritis. Her work is called primitive art, it has a simple and clear style...she had no formal training. She painted in a natural way, drawing from her memory and capturing American rural life. Grandma Moses viewed her art as something she enjoyed doing, not understanding why people paid such high prices for her pictures. Paintings which she first sold for about $5 later were sold for $8,000 to $10,000. In November 2006, her work "Sugaring Off", became her highest selling work at $1.2 million. Enjoying phenomenal success, she was honoured by Presidents and Governors. Several books have been written about her. A "Grandma Moses Day was proclaimed in New York and she appeared on the cover of Time and Life Magazines and on millions of greeting cards. A US commemorative stamp was issued in her honour in 1969. She lived to be 101 and in the last year of her life painted twenty-five pictures. Here, we would like to mention her famous quote *"Life is what we make it, always has been, always will be"*.

Harry Bernstein : Harry Bernstein, by the time he was 24, he had published a short story in a magazine. That was in 1934. He would then face the rejection of more than 40 novels over seven decades before he achieved literary success again. At the age of 96, Harry Bernstein published his memoir "The Invisible Wall". He wrote the manuscript for the "Invisible Wall" when he was 93 as a way to deal with his memories and the loneliness he felt after his wife's death of almost seven decades, Ruby passed away from leukemia in 2002. Spending his nights alone thinking of her as well as his rough childhood, the book deals with the anti-Semitic and bigotry his family suffered while he was growing up in a Lancashire mill town in north-west England. The strength of his prose has often been compared to the works of D.H. Lawrence and Frank McCourt. He has published two more books. The Dream and The Golden Willow. He recently celebrated his 100th birthday on May 30, 2010 and is now working on a fourth book. According to Harry Bernstein *"I realised then why I had failed in writing novels, because I turned away from personal experience and depended on imagination."*

Nola Ochs : Nola Ochs on May 14, 2007 became a Guinness Book of World Record holder as the world's oldest college graduate. The 95-year old graduated from Fort Hays State University in Kansas 77 years after she first started taking classes. She earned a general studies degree with an emphasis in history, graduating alongside her grand daughter who was 21 years old at the time. She always loved learning, but got a little sidetracked. "I live on a farm. I was a mother, grand mother, great grand mother." I had plenty to do. But the yearning didn't go away. So, after her husband died in 1972, she started taking correspondence courses again. Slowly, she is plugging away at her Bachelors Degree. She then spent the last year in a dorm for non-traditional students working on her general studies degree. She says *"I came here with no thought of it being an unusual thing at all. It was something I wanted to do. It gave me a feeling of satisfaction."*

George Burns : George Burns Actor, comedian, writer. His career spanned almost the entire 20th century. At the dawn of recordings, movies and television, he was one of the pioneers who helped invent modern show business. From Vaudeville, he was able to make the transition to modern show business by keeping his act current with the times. Achieving legendary status, he could still get in there and mix it up. After the death of his beloved wife Gracie, he started appearing in movies again. He also did one-man shows to pack houses, getting better as he got older. He won an Academy Award for Best Supporting Actor in Neil Simon's "The Sunshine Boys" at the age of 79, the oldest recipient for that award.

When he was approaching his eighties, he decided to start putting his wit and wisdom down on the printed page. The man who barely finished the fourth grade, ended-up writing eight books - all of them best sellers including a marvelous tome of the love of his life, entitled Gracie: A Love Story. According to George Burns *"I'd rather be a failure at something I love than a success at something I hate."*

There are hundreds of such examples of success. In whatever stage of life you are right now, you will need your soul's guidance in future. Your soul will always try to give you some hints. It will continue doing its work. You will have to act on it right then. You have to do your work according to your soul's voice. Soul will keeps on telling you again and again till you are alive. It is its nature. You can do anything if you want. But first you should be friends with your soul. Listen to its appeal, make a promise in your heart. Find your positives and negatives. The reason of your negatives are not knowing your soul properly. All these negatives gradually come into your unconscious mind. Your soul works 95 per cent and the rest five per cent depends on action. In comparison to your soul, your actions do not have that much of strength. When a child sees his father having alcohol and cigarette, he also starts taking it. He doesn't realise that he is getting into a bad habit. We have discussed before also that these negatives don't come in you from your birth. You were born pure and simple at that time. You acquired these negatives from your environment and slowly these negatives became the part of your personality. When you will build a relationship with your soul be friendly with it, these negatives will vanish one by one. The day you start doing good, you will feel light within yourself. You will be free from this false world, show-off and bragging attitude. And believe me your life will start changing.

Disciplined Life

You need a certain kind of discipline to do any kind of work. If you have desire to make a relationship with your soul than discipline and planning will come into your life automatically. We have to listen to God's massage, make a promise and take action. When you start doing this, members of your family, friends and everybody around you might laugh at you. People will try to stop you. That is natural. These are signs of your success and we get to know who all are jealous of you. Your success is beyond their comprehension. They can not do what you are doing. What you have chosen is very important and is God's wish. If you have chosen this path according to God's wish, then you will not have to change it ever. When you succeed in the end, everybody praise you. We want to ask you that did Shaheed Bhagat Singh change his way. Did Mahatma Gandhi change his way? This is the right way, in spite of being they are lone fighter. You just have to keep your focus on yourself. This will give you more strength and internal peace. And the realisation of it come soon when you start feeling light and good about yourself. You will be nearer to your goal. This is not only good for you but also good for people who are working with you. You will find a good feeling inside you will know that you are on the right path. It doesn't matter that whether you have reached to great heights or not but you will start feeling a strong determination inside you which will tell you that you can reach to your destination. This can take time but victory is surely come to your way one dayl. You will start feeling this all is possible only because of soul awareness. You will start attracting people who have the same kind of zeal and enthusiasm. You will take your project to its final stage. When you reach this stage you will feel that your soul is becoming powerful day by day. You will get immense strength. Your self-confidence will increase then you will be in a position to do all kind of works which many successful people have done in their eventful life.

The results will be in a way you never imagined. You will not depend on anybody and you will not expect anything from anybody. The kind of works which seemed impossible earlier will start getting attractive now. You will be free from jealousy and hatred. You will love yourself and will respect yourself. You will start accepting yourself the way you are. Your nature will be similar to your soul's nature. The way your soul leads a free life. similarly you will also live freely. Only knowledge can give you peace, acceptance and support.

This is the only way to develop a healthy relationship with this world. For example, you will agree that all small and big action we take in our daily life is not according to our thoughts for that we need a proper planning. You get angry almost ten times in a day. After knowing your soul you will get angry may be on few times. If you do this there will be some changes can be seen in your behaviour. You will notice it and you will feel happy. Slowly, this will come to nought. Now, you might get angry once in ten or in 30 days. But people, who see you getting angry even in thirty days, will think that you still get angry. You don't have to worry about that. You will feel proud of the small achievements you have made. You will get rid of bad habits like hatred, jealousy, injustice, cruelty, ego, betrayal and meanness etc. Your small achievements will give birth to good habits inside you. You will start to follow the right path. You will be educated, well-informed and aware about your soul in the right manner. After doing all this you will get a healthy life and this will be a proof that you are on the right way. Your face will always have natural smile and not like the artificial smile of an air hostess. You will feel some difference in your personality. You will feel that you are always encouraged for doing good work. Realities of life will attract you and your life will give you internal peace. You try to understand things in your own way. You welcome each day with new energy. Your life now feels a lot of freshness. You become more sensitive. After knowing all this, don't you think that you should trust your soul? You have never seen your soul. There will always be a new answer whenever you meet your soul.

Avoid Hypocrisy

We want to say one more thing related to your soul. One should save himself from being divided into two parts. You must have seen that people believe in some specific thoughts and conviction. But under the pressure of society, they agree to do something which is not according to their conviction and voice of their soul. You can say it is a double standards and hypocrisy. We should strongly believe in our thoughts and should stick to our principles.

Here, we would like to share one good example with you. **Mr Saxena** is a very sober person. His wife is too a pious lady and used to practice lot of religious activities and rituals. Every week she goes to temple for offering her prayers to God. Though Mr Saxena believes in almighty God and he thinks that God is present in everywhere. Having these kinds of thoughts he does not feel like going to temple every week. But he cannot say 'no' to his wife and goes to temple every week without his wish. What will you say to this situation? According to common perception this is a double standard. If he does not believe in any kind of ritual and religious act then why he is going with his wife? He should speak through his heart and tell her wife honestly what he feels. This is wrong on the one hand you are unwillingly supporting someone's thought process and top of that you are not honest to yourself. You will find generally people behave like that and they do not reach anywhere in life because they do not have courage to speak truth.

For example cine star **Salman Khan** says in the context of one of his movies "Once I commit to do something then I don't even listen to myself." We don't know how much people understood this. The meaning of this sentence is, till a person doesn't want to do anything himself, nobody can force him. He sticks to his principles; if he doesn't do it he can never be successful. He should save himself from being divided into two parts. He will live his life fully and develop a deep relationship with his soul. Through this divine knowledge a man will not only lead a balanced and simple life but will live life on his basic principles. You have God's element inside you. It is better for you to find it so that eternal goodness can prevail in your life and change it forever.

We can compare our soul with a traffic police officer. The officer controls the traffic, which goes in different directions. If we consider traffic as desires, you will be able to understand the role of soul easily. If the traffic police officer does not control the traffic properly. There will be too much of chaos and jam for hours on the road.

We can compare soul with the ereee referee of the match. You cannot play a match without the referee. If you do this no team will be able to play properly and the match will not finish with a proper outcome. Now, you imagined how you can live a healthy and successful life without your soul.

Work Harmoniously

The biggest motive of life is the meeting of soul and mind. When these two meet they complement each other and give the feeling of wholeness. When body, mind and soul work harmoniously in a tandem one can expect unbelievable positive results.

Find the truth and work for others selflessly. If you are burdened with your life's problems your mind will not function properly. Man things how to get out of this problem. Sometimes, you see a dividing line between the body and mind. This is a known fact that all your body parts function through your mind only. If you surrender in body's weakness, laziness, and lethargic feeling, in that case this dividing line becomes thick in your mind and all positive and creative thoughts get out of your systems. Your way to go ahead is stopped. If you don't want to have this dividing line in your mind you will have to fill every day of your life with new energy and thoughts. Your mind is full of today's problems. It has a desire to generate more money to copy others and to go ahead. We cannot remove all this things from our mind even if we want to. Here the role of soul becomes very big. How to get a new massage in your life? How to attain peace? How to find the right work? How to win over disappointments? There are many questions like this whose answers are hidden in your own soul.

If you will consume too much alcohol, you will involve yourself in nasty relationship. This results in over-working of your broken and disappointed mind. But if you have a determination to do something new then 90 per cent of your work is done. It all depends on how strong is your own determination to your desired work done.

There is another thing that you should understand. If you believe that the world which is full of rituals is your ideal, then you should take out this believe from your mind. Eating food is a necessity of your body, but to be a proper human being you need the awareness of your soul. Happiness for us is a complete life with determination, dedication and seriousness. As soon as you reach heights of satisfaction, new doors will open for you. This feeling will be the strongest of feeling you have felt till now.

By doing this, you will find a new kind of happiness. You will discover surprising good things in you will encourage you towards humanity. This will bring Goutam Budhha and Jesus Christ to your level and will take you to their level. These desires will generate a new power inside you which will take you to complete accomplishment. Passion is already inside you and that is your birth right. You just have to realise your passion and work accordingly. See in case of the great sage Mahatma Buddha whose unbridled passion made him leave a very comfortable life to attain salvation (*nirvana*).

4

How to Connect with Your Soul

Take Right Decision

Let's discuss that if a person hears his inner-voice of soul before going to do any work, he not only will get complete success and peace but even society will be benefitted at large. You must be surprised that how it is possible? Let's discuss this in detail. If a person hears the voice of his soul and understands it then he will move towards a direction where he will get hundred per cent success. Hearing your inner-voice means following God's command. You can be sure that you cannot go wrong. To recognise the right path choose it and follow it with firm resolve and determination without getting distracted in difficult situations is a sign of a successful personality.

First, a man should understand his right path. He faces with lot of options and problematic situations. He gets confused and doesn't know in which way he should proceed. In such a situation, his advisers are his family members, friends and parents, etc., who have their own opinions and their own believes. A man should listen to everybody but must take right decision judiciously which involved all the practicalities of life. If he does this his success is definite. Whatever views his family got about him are because of their own environment and their value system they are brought-up in. They used to keep living in that system and do not achieve anything remarkable. They will give their opinions what is right for them. But it is not important that their opinion are right for you also, because your education, environment, thoughts, values and believes are different than them. Your goal in life is different than theirs. So, if you want to take an important decision in your life then you will have to save yourself from being misled. One should take that right direction in his life which has the consent of his internal soul. It has been seen in lot of situations, a man feels weak because of his children, family and cannot decide what to choose out of it. There will always be challenges in selecting a right path which is encouraged only by your soul. This is because you have not chosen an easy way but when you start walking on it you will feel yourself that there is no way easier than this. This is the way of truthfulness. Way of truth is always full of challenges but if a person can take up challenges and not run away from them, only he can be successful. His confidence and strength is visible to all. He doesn't ask anything from anybody and has the courage to say whatever is right. He has a feeling of equality for all. He doesn't follow the world but make his own path. He is always seeing different from the crowd. People make fun of him and oppose him initially but after his success they respect him and agree with him. His becomes an inspiration to others. He gets money, fame, respect what may not which he ever imagined. His life is filled with happiness forever. You will see many examples in and around the world but why does this happen? This proves the same points that one, who hears the voice of his soul, follows it. Only, he is fortunate enough to get all of this. We should think that the role of the soul is so extraordinary that no success is possible without it. Then why didn't we try to understand soul?

Understanding of Soul

Let's discuss this now. We do this because when we are doing something after listening to our inner-voice, we can be rest assured that this is the massage of God. When God chooses somebody to execute a certain kind of work, he chooses with something in his mind. What we mean is in normal families work is always given to a responsible person. If you give work to an irresponsible person, there will be no results. If God has chosen you to do something, think how much capability and talent he must have seen in you. Then why do people ignore soul's voice? If you have chosen your work according to God's will, then you will have to imbibe many qualities such as honesty, not hurting any body, truthfulness, no alcohol, no non-vegetarian food and no unethical way. We have to get rid of all these bad habits. It is very difficult to leave all of them. You face lot of disappointments and difficulties because of these habits but still you don't leave them. You can not get rid of such addictions easily. These addictions can be treated under the guidance of proper organisation. It will help you to get rid of this situation. Everybody wants to get rid of addictions but 99 per cent are unable to get rid of their addictions though they want badly. Have you ever thought why that is so? Generally, such type of people are very weak from inside. Because, they haven't got enough love and affection in their life where they brought-up. They easily get tempted to such addictions and become the slave of these bad habits.

You don't even listen to your soul's inner-voice before doing your work. By doing this, your soul gets weaker and weaker day by day and affects your performance at the place of work, characters and health to put you in the state of total disarray. You lose your prestige to lose confidence in the market. People do not believe you. On the other hand, the work which you do with the consent of your soul will take you towards success. Your soul also be strengthened and you generate lot of satisfaction and peace in life.

Now, the question arises that whether a normal man is ready for all this or not. Today there are so many disoriented ways of life. People are unable to discard temptation. Alcohol is easily available everywhere, too much of non-vegetarian food. People are after unnatural sex and prostitution. Who will be able to save himself in such an environment? People are caught up in swamp due to these bad habits. But there are good people also who are usually not getting tempted to all these things. They are happy, physically and mentally healthy, and achieve a great amount of success in their life. The way they adopted after hearing the voice of their inner-soul may be full of challenges but when they get success it is rejoicing for them also. If a person has determination and he wants to forsake his bad habits he can do that if he tries whole-heartedly but the problem is everybody doesn't want to tread on this difficult path. Everybody wants to get successful by adopting various ways and think that the success will come to them automatically like a miracle.

Be Patient

If you listen to your inner-voice with patient and great care and work according to it from that moment your journey of inner happiness gets started. This is the beginning of becoming a good human being. You just have to listen to your soul and there will be so many good things that will come to you that you will not be able to count. For example, Thomas Alva Edison discovered electricity, now you see, there are so many things attached to electricity. You have fan, cooler, motor, freeze, television, washing machine, internet etc. so many things which are used by electricity. Thomas Alva Edison made our life very easier and simple. But without electricity there is no use of all these devices. Therefore, for a moment you consider your soul is electricity. Soul in the form of electricity is that voice which will attach many good features in your personalities. Our mind and body all have so much of strength that they can invent various new devices.

You must have heard in general saying i.e., "where there is a will there is a way". If you have a strong will of developing a wonderful relationship with your soul, you will get a way to reach there. If you have this feeling in your heart that you have to meet your soul, it is enough to be the first step in this enchanting journey. Till now we have discussed knowing your soul and not being able to develop a relationship with it. In this chapter, we will learn how to develop a relationship with your soul.

To do this first and foremost we have to come in the role of a student. If we follow the ethics of the students, first you need to educate yourself and should be develop a very strong urge within you. You will have to understand the difference between a discipline student and indiscipline student. First, we will talk about discipline student. When a child become the student his name is written in a school, his uniform and books are bought. He has a time to go to the school. He studies there for a definite period of time. What he has to study there, is already decided by his teacher. He studies something new every day. Gradually, he feels that he is learning something new and sees a change inside himself. If he does this all while being a very discipline student, then he is surely a good student.

Now, let's talk about an indiscipline student. He never goes to school on right time. Often he goes school not in proper uniform and also he is not present always in the class. During the school hours, he goes to movies or clubs by bunking the classes. He drinks and misbehaves with his mates. He is also a student. His name is also written in the school records but is he following the code of conduct of students which he should be? Is he learning what is important for his life? Is he true to himself? Do you think he will be able to apply his half-baked knowledge in his life?

If we look into our life we find that we study good things to improve ourselves in our practical life. Sometimes, we try to understand few things but we do not work on those things remaining in our role in our students. If we want to develop a relationship with God then we have to learn the lessons of life like a good and obedient student. We have to learn new things. We have to inculcate new habits in our behaviour whatever is necessary to develop a beautiful relationship with our soul. We have to understand all those things and we have to bring them in our behaviour of daily life. You can take a break if you are ill or not well someday. But be committed to yourself. You are your own teacher. You are your own principal and student. Nobody will come and ask you to do anything. You are your own boss and improve yourself. You might find this a little awkward, but if you have to bring a change in your life, this is the only way. Let's discuss those things which are important in developing a relationship with your soul.

Practice Meditation

The first job you have to do is that to meditate daily for ten minutes. You should understand the seriousness of meditation and learn it from a knowledgeable *Guru*. By meditation we mean that you relax your body, mind and brain completely. Focus on your heart and mind tries to talk to God daily. It is important to be friendly with God. You have to develop a connection with him. Whatever promise you do with yourself, follow it with full conviction and honesty. You have to give attention to all your actions and become your own critic. Kabir said wonderfully describing this situation...

"Bura jo dekhan mai chala, bura na milya koy, jo dil khoja aapna mujhse bura na koi" means when I went out

to see negative qualities of life in the outer world, I could find none. When I peeped inside myself, I was the bad one.

When you peep inside your deep down then you become the biggest critique of yours. To be on the right track, you have to find critic, friends so that they can point out your mistakes rather than praising you on your face for every type of action all the time. We can mention here a beautiful couplet of Saint Kabir:

"Nindak niyare rakhiye aangan kuti chawaye, bin pani sabun bina nirmal kare subhaye." Means be surrounded by your critique and true friends, they will pin point your mistakes and it will help you to grow in life.

If you start follow this thought process in your daily routine and make small promises to yourself everyday you will find that gradually a connect with your soul is established. For that you need to do *yoga* daily without any excuse you have to do it religiously. The meaning of *yoga* is to connect with you. You need to connect your heart, brain and soul together. If you cannot balance these three important parts of your body together the better result will not be seen. This is necessary because today's life is so busy and it is natural to lead an imbalanced life. Today man has created confusion and complications for himself. He is caught up in these complications and cannot blame anybody for that. There is a major distraction and no connection with his heart and brain. If we talk about soul, people do not have time to think about their soul for a second whereas knowing your soul is the most important things than anything else.

Practice Yoga

When you do *yoga,* you concentrate on your body parts like heart, brain and soul. You give these body parts a due importance that is required and necessary. You need to become your own friend and learn to respect yourself. When you will unite your body parts together to function then only you can connect with your own soul. By doing *yoga* your arteries, blood vessels and body become flexible and you will feel active and energetic. You will feel like doing your work efficiently. The blood flow in your brain will be smooth and function properly. We have found from one case study that we use only four per cent of our brain, genius use 10 per cent of their brain. Rest 90 per cent is unused.

Extraordinary people believe firmly on their thoughts. They do their work with full conviction without thinking about people and make best use of their brain. Your life can also be changed forever if you will use your brain maximum in the right direction.

Pranayam

Along with *yoga,* you need to connect yourself with *Pranayam. Yoga* and *pranayam* will bring spirituality in your life. *Pranayam* is an exercise of breaths. In many situations, our body is like a dead body, but breaths never stop and are running since we have taken birth on this earth. The cycle of breaths never breaks and when it will break we will not be alive anymore. It means these breaths are a form of God that is flowing in our body. Through *pranayam* we take breath in and release our breaths out. By doing this our body function works smoothly and the flow of blood becomes proper. Your blood gets appropriate oxygen and you will feel fresh and energetic. Your immune system of body will improve and it will cure all your ailments. It will happen only when you will connect yourself with soul.

To connect with your soul, one need to control his food habits and will have to follow a certain kind of discipline. One needs to keep away himself from non-vegetarian foods, alcohol and drugs. One needs to eat good food timely.

He will have to avoid excess eating habits. It will be beneficial if you keep a fast on fix-day in a week. You need to eat only two times in a day morning and evening only. There should be at least eight hours of gap between these two meals. We often see the people are dying from access eating. We have not seen people dying with less eating. You need to keep an eye on your food habits closely. You need to think seriously what kinds of food you are eating. You should not have any toxic food and must have only healthy vegetarian diet. It may not be according to your taste only but it is essential to keep yourself healthy.

It is said *Jaisa khaye ann, waisa rahe tan man* Means the kind of food you will have, you will feel and become accordingly.

Food Habit

You must be wondering that why we are discouraging to have non-vegetarian food. We will try to give this answer. Suppose you are an energetic man and have got lot of money. You beat a poor man. Take everything from him. You kill his wife and children in front of his own eyes. Just think, will he bless you for your heinous crime? You will not have any idea how badly he will curse you from inside. Likewise, you will have to think about that innocent animal who cannot speak, who does not know the language but he knows you are going to kill him. He will curse you from inside and its body will be affected with that ill-feeling. Our body is made from millions of cells. The body of animal is also made from millions of cells. After you will kill that animal its cursed body cells will be full of awful feeling. If you will eat that flesh it is sure that meat will make you sick because that animal was being killed without any mercy only for your taste of tongue which is for a very short period of tasteful enjoyment. If you realise consciously with full awareness you will find the taste of meat till it rolling in your mouth and as long as it touches with your tongue. The moment you swallow that piece there is no taste left behind. There is no taste before and after swallowing it. Don't you think is it momentary? And people are killing innocent animal for their taste and for unwanted bad food habits. Your power and bad taste of eating become the reason for its killing. You eat non-vegetarian food for your taste only. The consumption of animal meat will add ailment and affect your heart and liver. It will raise your blood pressure and it will increase your anger. If you think that non-vegetarian food will give you energy and strength then you are living in fool's paradise.

We want to tell you that the symbol of power is horse but the horse is purely vegetarian. Now, you take the decision by yourself that you want to correct your food habits or not? Or you still want to have non-vegetarian food for your taste.

If you want to be a free and independent person then you have to make a strong connection with your soul. You have to become owner of your own. Boss of your own, means you will do your work freely and with full honesty and truthfulness. Do your work with full freedom. Nobody will be there to interfere in your work. When you are forcibly doing something it means you are not doing that work with full honesty, because you are doing that work against your will. By doing so, you are doing injustice with yourself. If you will perform your duties well the result will always be good and in your favour. When you are performing boss of your own it doesn't mean that you should misuse your power, brain and money. A doctor has knowledge to save a patient's life. It is entirely up to him whether he will cure him and give life or will he give him death? What we are trying to say is one need to make use of his knowledge, money and power for humanity. While doing any work there has to be hundred per cent consent of your body, heart, brain and soul. In a nutshell, you need to control yourself and take decision in life.

Now, you have to work on your own ideas, you need to spend money and times on those ideas and accept challenges while implementing your ideas. You should gamble on your own ideas. You must be wondering to hear this how will you gamble? And why you should gamble? Let's understand this, have you ever noticed when you were taking any decision, in a way you do the gambling. For example, if you are marrying some female you never know will that marriage work? But you gamble. What will you get end of the day that is entirely up to that particular decision? If you closely see your decision, it is a gamble. One needs to play on his own thought. When you are marrying someone you need to fix your priorities. You may be failure in that marriage but it is sure that you will not be regretting rather feel contented on your own decision. You need to take risk in life but it should be calculative and thoughtful risk. Kindly, don't mistaken us we are only telling you not teaching you. Gamble is the human nature of every human being. It is deep rooted in us. If people failed in any work or business they keep blaming their destiny. Often they talk about their failure among public.

One needs to take his failure in a positive manner. He should think in a way that "he has not failed, the work he has chosen to do have failed", he will have to think that his success is hidden in some other work and he needs to find that to do with the help of soul.

Addiction

One need not to be intoxicated himself. You must be wondering it is always advisable that one need to keep away from all kinds of intoxication but why we are saying this? Now, we will try to understand this point in detail. You must have found around you that somebody has an addiction of singing, some has listening of song, somebody has an addiction of serving people, and somebody has to earn more and more money. Film-maker has an addiction of making films. An artist has an addiction of his art, writer has writing addiction, some has the addiction of maintaining good health, somebody wants to make mega structure building, someone wants to go on top of the Himalaya, some thinks that he will go on the moon. You must have understood what we are trying to say and where we are pointing out. Now, just think about drinking alcohol, offering drinks to friends will help someone? This unnatural intoxication will be for few hours. Do you think it can give permanent peace and happiness? This is not a natural intoxication or addiction. Can you describe this in front of people? No. Here we want to say this intoxication or addiction is natural in human nature. Addiction is necessary and natural but it should not be physical, unnatural and toxic. It should exist in us internally with feeling and emotion.

Creative mental intoxication is permanent. It gives pleasure. Physical intoxication or addiction is temporary. It is quite possible that it can give you momentary happiness but it has no legitimate effect. If you will build up a divine relationship with your soul then only you will get to know about that natural addiction within you. You will discover this new thing in you and thank your God. You will create a deep bound with your soul because to discover this unknown creative venture you followed the instruction of soul.

Purity and Sincerity

You need to become a bold person to make a relationship with your soul. You need to fight to improve your bad habits. Fight for goodness, peace and prosperity. If you want to be happy tomorrow then from today onwards you need to live a life with purity and sincerity. Like gamble and intoxication, fighting is also a human nature.

It is natural. In a nutshell, man got a fighting nature from his birth.

We will take two examples from the history. You must have read or heard about emperor **Ashok** and the incident of mindless killing in Kalinga war. When emperor Ashok saw countless dead bodies of the soldiers all around just after the war, his soul jolted him. There were several questions that were bothering him like, what had he done or what he gained by doing this? Why had he done this? Why this war was fought? What was he going to achieve with the killing of soldiers. He caught in this web found him guilty. He considered his guilt was so mindless and inhuman that he couldn't sleep many nights after that. He was not getting peace anywhere. His soul was stiring him with several questions again and again. He had no answer for what he had committed and that too willingly in the hopes becoming a powerful king. That repentance transformed him completely and later on, he changed his path to become the true followers of Gautam Buddha and that too, forever. He engaged his influence to serve the cause of humanity. He had spreaded the great message of the Buddha religion all over the world. After this incidence, he never fought war and completely surrendered himself to feet of Buddha.

Geeta Gyan

In second example, lord Krishna gave the preaching of *Geeta Gyan* to Arjuna and cleared his doubts. He told Arjuna whom you are considering your close one's are all dead. Your grandfather, uncle, *Guru* and your brother all are on the wrong path. They are not with "*dharma*" they look physically alive but mentally have already died. Lord Krishna described further that that is why "Hey Arjuna" don't be emotional and perform your duty as a great worrier and finish this "*Adharm*a" on this earth and establish 'Dharma'. You have got ability and you are a brave worrier and the best in your field. If they can do injustice to you, just think it over for a moment, will they spare normal human being? They will create hell for them. That is why you have to play your role in this "*Dharma Yudh*". They are misusing their constitutional power. You have to understand that the power does not corrupt people may be the base for corruption is ultimately people corrupt power. You will have to finish their constitutional power to save this earth. This is your duty which you have to perform. Arjuna has understood and followed Lord Krishna's way and philosophy and established "*Dharma*" by killing Kouravas in Mahabharata.

In both these examples, there are fights but both are different in nature. Fighting is man's nature from ages. In both the situation, you will find soul played an important role. The great emperor Ashok was jolted down by his soul and he became the followers of Buddha forever. He must have fought with himself and adopted Buddha religion. On the other hand, Lord Krishna helped Arjuna by telling him truth about body and soul and further explained to fight for the justice and rightesousness.

5

Forms of Soul and its Power

Firm on Principle

While talking about soul, it is necessary to avoid the division of a human personality. One must have observed that though people believe in a thought of positive attitude but due to social pressure they succumb to the pressure which doesn't gel well to their personality. They don't believe in certain principles but want to present a goody goody image. For example, you live in a city. People look up to you. They respect you. Suppose a rich man's son manhandled a poor guy. Police put him behind the bars. This case presumably comes to you to bail him out. Some people known to both sides plead for his bail.

You are in a dilemma to be on the side of justice or not if you bail him out to win the goodwill, it will be called a hypocrite. Man should remain committed to his stand-point, belief and conviction.

In this world no one can be forced to do anything till he convinced himself but he has to remain firm on his principle. If one doesn't follow this principle, he will not be a gainer in this game.

People do not go by their soul's instructions instead they follow social and environmental norms. If you are sure and do something against your feeling, it is sure that this will torture you whole life. You will lose trustworthiness. You will start disobeying your soul and ethical values. Thus, your soul and mental power start getting lessen. Apart from that you will start losing your self-respect among society. If you can not respect yourself how you get respect from your known circle? You will lose your control on yourself and work in indiscipline manner. Thus, you will not achieve desired success for that almighty has created you. You will lose position in the society and it is a strong possibility that you may indulge in various criminal activities.

You should avoid indecision. You cannot force anyone till one himself agrees to that point of view. But for this, he has to remain firm on his principle without this, nothing positive will emerge. You can't have best of all the worlds all the time by a firm conviction. A man will live a total life and will form a unique relationship with spirituality. He will be an ideal for himself. He will present a good example for the society at large. But many people are scared. They get distracted from their principles. If you are in spiritual state we will live by values. Your lifestyle will be total and ideal. You will explore the soul element in yourself which will change your nature and eventually your own life.

Self-controlled Energy

Soul is powerful as it is an inspired and energised force. It is active. It runs on a self-controlled energy. If you can identify it that you also get connected to such a supreme power which takes your personality to perfection, giving it a new meaning and making it bold.

You must be looking at sun-rising every morning. Have you ever assessed its power and energy? Giving the light to the whole world that life runs the life around us. It has its own energy which is active and self-controlled. If you also can identify the sun apparent in your soul and feel its power and energy then you will be able to pinpoint your shortcomings. You fear the darkness and not the light. You should identify this powerful form of the soul. If you want to go ahead in life you have to overcome your fear. Soul gives a man the boldness because he has the capacity and energy. Above all the soul is pure always.

One of the forms of the soul is happy to go lucky it reflects happiness, pleasure, laughter, guffaw, boldness, daring, carefree, and active. You must have observe that all happy go lucky people have these qualities. Such people are generally successful. Have you ever thought, why, because they are not dead? They live a bold life without any hypocrisy. They follow their soul. It is natural that their soul has this nature. You don't have to convince your soul like you do to your mind, heart and brain. It makes you feel its influence itself. It is a question of forming a relationship. Soul speaks itself you may touch it or not. It gives response properly, and convincingly. If you can make your life happy, go-lucky there will be total change in your life. You will meet people with smile. They will accept you with open arms by getting connected with you. They will consider your personality as an idealist. You will be able to fulfill your resolution. Your personality will become like a rock. Mind is wavering. It is never at peace with itself. You must understand soul is the key to life. It has an answer to all your questions. Soul is stable and there is no confusion.

Soul is Creator

Soul is creative in nature. When God is the biggest creator of this world then soul also is a divine part. How can soul be not creative when you enter a profession at the call of your soul then you add creativity with novelty. Common businessmen don't identify that novelty. They can't see through your actions and try to follow you. The motivational speaker Shiv Khera has said "a successful man is different in his every action" if you analyse this it means what you have chosen at the call of your soul an ability it will have the concurrence of your heart, mind and soul. It is like worship while doing this you get the feeling of pride. Suppose, till now you had no mental peace in whatever you did. Now you run such a restaurant which you wanted to have for long but you thought it was a minimal job. It won't take you anywhere. It was the voice of your soul. Now, you followed your mind. First of all you will give it a unique design may listen the echo of good feelings.

You will improve the quality of dishes that are liked by customers and keep them healthy. You will attract the same customers again and again. You can't be creative without listening to your soul if you form a relationship with your soul then this creative nature can make your life meaningful.

Soul is Infinite

The power of soul is infinite, if you want to bring a positive change there is no option then to form a relationship with it. Even if a man desires he can't change himself automatically. Sometime we try to change others but they argue with you. Generally, wavering mind create indecision and breaks even firm resolution. Human life oscillates like a pendulum because it follows his heart and mind both guide his decision. Today's man has forgotten the role of soul in his life. He presumes the soul is a devilish secret of life and death. He doesn't want to talk about it but what is interesting here you can't take correct decisions without identifying the soul. It creates total anarchy. Sheer heart and mind can't give successful results in the long run. However, if there is consent of soul the result will be successful in the long run, in the interest of humanity and even give a correct decision to your life. One, who connects to his soul he is aware of the elements. Therefore, in the final analysis there can't be a fundamental change in your life without the consent of soul.

Soul's nature is also momentary and spontaneous. It can change your life in a moment. It happened in the life of many great people. Even in the business of successful entrepreneurs. For example, Thomas Alva Edison saw the lightening one-day and he made research to know the reason of it and discovered electricity. When and apple fell on Newton's head he was forced to think why it fell down and not went up. He threw a ball in air again and again as it also came down in the same way. It ultimately led Newton to discover the important principle of gravitational attraction. All big inventions are the result of this momentary nature. Emperor Ashok changed his heart after the Kalinga war. It was the voice of his soul. Lord Budhha's renunciation is also a product of the soul. Dacoit Angulimal was changed because of his soul. History is full of such examples. The permanent and pure nature of soul led to extra ordinary achievements. We have seen it all.

Soul is Playful

Soul is also playful. It enjoys life. Lord Krishna did all great things in his playful nature. Two lovers become life-long partners after a casual beginning. Many a time it is difficult to find a suitable boy or a girl for marriage in the world at large but we stumble upon a suitable match without making any special efforts for it. Even in business, you try hard. Nothing happens but you take decision casually and succeed. Generally, soul contributes 95 per cent in such cases.

There are thousand of examples in our society, even illiterate and uneducated people are highly successful because of their soul power. On the other hand, you will find well-educated and trained people from well-known university are failed because they have not given due importance to their soul power.

Decisive

The nature of soul is decisive. You must over heard kids. They have a special innocence. They take decision easily in a jiffy because they are devoid of the worldly craftiness. Despite their brain, heart and mind are not fully developed, they listen to their soul. When you form a relationship with your soul, then it is free of all deceit. This quality of soul enters in your system and helps you to move forward. The decisive power of the soul and your noble behaviour lead you to extraordinary success. You can't think of them ordinarily.

Alert Soul

Soul is always alert in perfect shape. Alertness also includes knowledge. One, who is alert and is aware about soul. It is always active and alert at work and round the clock. Man seeks half of the time in fact even when awake he works half-heartedly. In such a situation how can you expect unexpected success? Without knowing the deep-rooted element of knowledge of life you cannot form relationship with the soul. In fact, most of us do not know what knowledge is though they claim otherwise. No great person in history has made such a claim in fact they submit it the acquired knowledge for humanity still they led a student's life. Those who have formed a relationship with soul only, they achieved the basic element.

Soul's nature is not limited. It is expanding every day. It goes up and up every moment. That is its nature. One, who is limited in thought his total perspective will be small and narrow. You must have met people who are self-content they remain cut off. They want to hide their shortcomings. They cut off from the society. They don't accept their shortcomings. They don't want to talk about. Often they suffer from inferiority complex. If you love your soul then your behaviour can not be changed. When a tree grows its size, makes people realise that it is big. Lot of people can rest under its shadow. Man's personalities also like that he should try to attain big heights. This is possible only with soul. He can reach the top peaks with this nature.

Unique Soul

Soul is infinite in its nature and is unique also. It is multifarious, exhaustive and dominating. When a man listens to his soul and makes resolve to change himself he finds everyday in a new shape and he feels an intense spiritual knowledge. Nothing can come out without it only alertness, completeness and communication and come with intense knowledge. Man gets a new world view like this. His conservative superstitions get uprooted in their place. Progressive values and new believes inspire him to go ahead. Man rediscovers himself. You can reach the truth by looking deep into yourself. You will always speak truth. You will become truth personified. You will become more competent and you will not get involved in trivia. When you become the master of your all senses this state is ultimate realisation. It takes a man to in totality after this you can solve all problems. Every situation is the truth of its circumstances which different people adopt differently.

Soul is like **traffic police** that controls it. If red green and yellow lights are not followed there will be chaos. Nobody will be able to negotiate with the role. Senses are like these lights if police does not control these lights. It will be free for all. There will be total jam. Now, you must have realised how our senses create confusion. Obstructing thinking if police is not keeping alert it can't control traffic. Soul also gives correct direction to its senses. If soul does not direct you it will lead to jam and chaos. Therefore, it is necessary to be remained in the state of alertness.

Soul is like a **match referee**, you can't play without referee. Absence of referee leads to confuson. Consequently, it will make a negative impact on the proceedings of the match and the sportsmanship is also get insulted. Goodwill of the match will be affected. The players and referee on the field can entertain spectators by their good behaviour and sporting nature. Then a positive result can be expected. Referee changes it all by giving its unsporting nature. On the other hand if you think the ground was same so were the spectators only referee was a new one. The complexion of the game was totally changed. Earlier, it was a battle ground. Soul plays the same role in our life without setting a relationship with it. How can you live a happy and successful life sans the positive affect of soul?

Convergence of Body, Mind and Soul

The biggest purpose of our life is the convergence of body soul and mind. They are complementary to each other. They have to have infallible believe and unity also mutual respect. They are incomplete in the absence of each other. When they meet they become part of each other leading to totality and accomplish the desired goal. When body, soul and mind work in a tandem a man gets extra-ordinarily results. We should look for truth and adopt it. We should be honest with ourself and others. If you are disturbed your mind stops working. It doesn't work properly. Man wants to get out of it. You know why it happens? Have you ever thought why it happens? We are responsible for it. We can see a break in our mind. It is definite the mind decide all our action if you are tired, lazy or not interested then this break becomes wider. You get far away from your values. You can't move ahead. If you can stop this break your life will be new every day. We are generally worried. May be for more money to copy others, sense of revenge all this disturb us.

Soul has a bigger role here it can stop this break. The disturbed mind does not let anything enter inside. The vigilance of soul decides the state of mind. We face some important question every day. How to find new direction, satisfaction, proper work, overcoming frustration, expectation from love? Soul can answer these questions then and there.

If you are alcoholic or have bad company then life will get affected. You will get embroiled in these relationships. Your frustration will force you to remain there. You get involved deeper. If you are determined to do something new you have achieved 90 per cent. You have to be strong internally only soul can do that. Please throw away all orthodoxy. They have no meaning in life. Only temple worshiping won't help, even Kabir has said:

Pathar puje hari mile to main pujun pahar, tase to chaki bhali pees khaye sansar means "If by worshiping a stone you can get God then perhaps the grinder is much better which feeds the whole world". Kabir has said in another couplet,

"Kakar pathar jod ke masjid laye banay, ta chad mullah bang de kya bahra hua khuday"

The priest put stones together to make a mosque and now he is calling for the God is He deaf.

We should try to live a meaningful life by getting rid of orthodoxy. Knowledge of element should be the base. The orthodoxy might have been useful at some time but today in the world of advertising mobile and internet do they have any meaning?

Food is a biological need but a divine change is necessary to be a good human being. For us pleasure should mean a meaningful and purposeful life with seriousness and completion. As you will reach satisfaction new horizons will open. Your desire to reach them will be stronger than ever before. You will find a new pleasure. You will explore new secrets toward humanity. Such desires will light a new obsession through a divine power. It will make you complete. The soul and obsession will help you succeed and this success will give you peace, self-respect, recognition popularity and self-control. Your respect will be heightened. This is your fundamental right.

6

Challenging Your Beliefs and Opinions

Beliefs and Opinions

Beliefs and opinions are the two most important thoughts to shape up any human being's nature. These are the thoughts that lead your life and whatever you want to become in your life just because of these thoughts only. You often noticed because of these thoughts on the one hand people are leading a divine life and dedicatedly working for humanity on the other hand you will also find people are criminal and involved in various inhuman and criminal activities in the society. Why is that so? To find out these opinions and beliefs you need to find out the root cause of it, how these beliefs and opinions formed with time and you follow this thought process and achieved things accordingly. It may be negative and positive beliefs and opinions both.

Your beliefs and opinions are the result of your environment. As we have described earlier that when a child born, he doesn't born with good or bad habits and behaviour. Whatever he learns, he learns from his environment after taking his birth. First he sees things in his surrounded environment then he absorbs and after that he starts practicing it. While practicing these things in his life he gets to know lot of other things and formed his opinions and beliefs accordingly. According to environmental societal norms he creates his opinion and belief that what is wrong and right. It is a kind of slow and steady learning and it gets matured with time and that can not be changed over night.

Now, you must have understood why people are different in their nature and behaviour. Why people argue? Why they have different opinions? Why they do different work? It is the result of their environment. Those who are living with negative beliefs and opinions and struggling in their life, they need to introspect and challenge their beliefs and opinions. According to them, their beliefs and opinions may be correct but when we see the overall progress of these kinds of people we find that their life is stagnant and they are not able to do anything in life. Why is that so? Because, the main reason is they haven't thought over their beliefs and opinions. Now, the question is what is to be done to overcome your negative beliefs and opinions? Let's discuss one by one.

Objective in Life

First, of all you need to make your life purposeful. You need to see that what is your aim and objective in life? Generally, people are following their daily routine and do not know where they are heading in their life. You need to understand that why you have come to this earth? It has got a specific purpose. God has sent you to do something, to contribute something. That is why you need to find out the purpose of your life. Without the purpose you can't reach anywhere. Here, I want to share one example with you. Mr Malhotra was failed in his chit-fund business and almost on the road. But he was a responsible person. He had to take the responsibility of his three daughters, who were unmarried. He had to make the arrangement of their marriages. For that he needed money. He started new business of bra-making because it could be easily started in low budget. He had a specific purpose of his life then. He worked hard with complete dedication and God too blessed him after seeing his single-minded devotion to lead him to reap a rich harvest in the form of a successful businessman.

One needs to make a **mission** in his life. There should be some target and goal. Without vision and mission no organisation or individual can grow. If you do not know what is your goal then work without any purpose? Working for what? Just for the sake of only eating and sleeping. Is this the aim of your life? That should not be the aim but this is an unfortunate part that most of people are unaware about their target. You listen to your soul, get an instruction from their soul but you do act and make target of your life. When you will have a specific target of your life then you will not follow any other way. There will be a specific road and you work constantly to reach at your destination. You have to design a higher vision of your life and live with it, and then only you can achieve big success in your life.

Negative beliefs are those whom you want to hide knowingly and do not want to display publicly. To understand this point, we take some example from daily life. Can a drunker announce publicly that he drinks alcohol daily? He does that daily and he hides this bad habit knowingly from society. Now, the point is why he is doing that? Because, that is his firm believe that taking alcohol is not bad either. That is his belief which has comes from his environment. He must have seen people drinking in his own environment and must have formed opinion about alcohol at that point of time. Now, he drinks daily.

In another example, people think teasing a girl is OK and it is acceptable in society. Many people do that on road without realising that what that poor girl must be going through when they do practice this cheap action. That is not their fault it is the result of their environment. They have learnt this insensitive behaviour from their environment. Now, the point is that they need to examine their negative beliefs and start working on them. It will not happen in a day. You need to challenge your insensitive beliefs and improve your behaviour.

Apart from your negative beliefs and opinions you have to reject tempted offers that can lead you to the wrong directions. We often see people are not strong enough to lead their life spiritually. It is a known fact that in today's world temptation is every where, temptation for illegal sex, drinking and toxic food habits and bad company. It may distract you from your goal and take you to the wrong path. As a sincere person, you have to avoid and reject these temptations that can take you to the wrong path. You need to overcome these weak points so that you can not indulge yourself in any bad habits.

Introspect Self

Introspection is the key to get out of it. More of you should do introspection of yourself. More you do your introspection it will further improve your personality. You need to take new challenges and responsibilities in life, so that you can improve your personality. These responsibilities should be such that can take you to the newer heights. When you take them seriously and start working on them your life will go in upward direction and will get immense peace and happiness in your life. People who do not take responsibilities or avoid them can not learn anything. You have to make it a habit that you should take challenges in life. Then only things will work in your favour and it is not difficult if you start following your soul honestly.

It is a very pertinent point that you should have an insight about your judgement to accept it or reject it.

People are always in dilemma they neither can take a firm decision on their judgement nor have a vision or insight to reject it. It is great learning people who are clear in his approach they are successful. They do not stuck in between, in catch-24 situation. In both the situations, you are moving forward if you accept your decision or reject it. But surely you should not linger on in between. You often see people saying that "I have taken a wrong decision, my judgement was not correct" how can you take right or wrong decision? It is entirely up to your strong character and mind. You have to have a strong personality to take any decision on your judgement.

We should not avoid fear and you should not afraid of fear rather you should face it and overcome it. Fear has got immense power but you should not do any work under any kind of pressure if you will do this it is confirm that it will lead you towards wrong direction. In Jain's philosophy, this is the main point. They give *Abhaydan* means 'fearless life'. When you start accepting fear's power means you are becoming fearful in your nature. That is not the form of your soul. The soul is fearless, dynamic, living, playful and spontaneous.

Mood and Reality

There is difference between mood and reality. Mood is momentary and reality is permanent. Whatever you do it should be balanced. You should not do any work because of your mood feeling. Mood swing is natural in human nature but you can not take any decision in your mood swing. That is one state of mind which you learn how to overcome. You must have noticed that people saying "today my mood is for drinking" mood for long drive, mood for having non-vegetarian food, mood for visiting prostitute and so on. Why we are discussing this because it is not your permanent nature and often mistaken your mood with reality and do something weird. Understand the reality then act accordingly. It will always give you positive result.

Whatever points we are discussing if you do not meditate it will not work. Meditation means connecting yourself with God. With that supreme power that is universal and immortal. That is how you can focus yourself and can see your deep down within that what are your positive side and negative side in your behaviour. By doing regular meditation and *yoga* practice you can overcome your weaknesses and start improving your nature.

We have discussed till now the inner-beliefs and opinions to improve your personality. There are some outer challenges also that one need to follow and understand. We have said it many times in previous chapters that we need to find out the right work for you that should be according to your ability, interest and skills. For that you need to identify your soul and challenge your beliefs and opinion which put a hindrance in your way then only you can find a right profession for you.

You need to find out closely in your life that to whom you are interacting in your daily life? You need to observe your relationships. If these relationships are giving you stressful feeling then it is advisable that immediately you should leave them and move forward. You need to reduce stressful connection. It doesn't matter who they are, now the point is if they are not helping you to achieve your goal and giving stressful feeling all the time then how long you can carry them. There will be day when they will automatically be vanished from your life but till then there will be too late then why not today?

To get a higher success in your life there are some important points that you have to observe strictly. See whom you are surrounded by? Are they successful people or failure in their life? Are they depressed in life? Now the point is why they are depressed, there must be some reason behind it but the point is if you will start listening to those people then most of the time you will also be discussing depressing thing with them. By associating with these kinds of people you can't get motivation to do something great in your life.

You need to find people around you according to your choice. For example, if you want to become billionaire then you need to find billionaire friends. If you want to become film director then you should find film directors friends. If you want to achieve spiritual heights then find spiritual friends. In a nutshell, what you want to become find people and friends according to your choice and need. One day, you will notice that you also become like them yet different in your field.

Generous in Spirit

Be generous in your spirit and learn to create for yourself. Make it a habit. By doing this you will notice a different kind of change in your personality and you will feel more confidant. Then whatever you will do, will do with it by giving your best for the very purpose or goal which you have set. Believe us the day you will start doing this with your single-minded devotion and dedication people will start liking you. You will be popular and people will love and respect you.

You need to see your daily routine, if it is not set then you should start working on that also, you should adopt good sleeping habit, you need to do daily exercise. You can do *yoga* and meditation instead of doing other exercises. You need to make a fix time for your daily exercise. By doing this, the result will be outstanding.

Generally, as human being we expect other all the time to love us, care for us and respect us. When they are giving these things to us then we feel depressed and deserted. You also need to learn to respect yourself, to love you to care yourself. Why waiting for others to do this for yourself.

It is a well-known fact that if you will not respect yourself then who will respect you. You have to become your own parents like parents pamper their kids in same manner you should also pamper yourself. Think like that you are the father and mother for yourself. Now, in sum up you need to introspect and challenge your beliefs and opinions.

7

Not the Astrology and Superstitions but the Soul Makes Life Successful

Mumbo Jumbo

Only by taking a refuge in the soul, life can be made more meaningful and successful. Man knows this but he is not ready to accept it. In fact, a human being does not accept the existence of soul that is why after doing everything his life is not productive.

All of us carry the sweet and sour memories of the past. There are hopes which are borne out of concerns for the future but no one wants to have a realistic view of the present. It should be made clear to you whether do well or bad, your present thought process will shape your future. We generally find the people believe in stars, astrology and superstitions taking it as their route to success. They think this is the right way. They feel happy by adopting such type of things in their life. But while doing so people don't value their worth. They believe more in astrology and the associated with *mumbo jumbo.*

Everybody wants to lead a comfortable life. People don't want to do anything on their own but they desire to get everything. They feel their destiny will change one-day without making any effort. They want to achieve everything: name, fame and money etc. They spend their whole life like this way and never wake-up from their slumber. When they don't find any change or success in their life, they presume that their worshipping to God do not yielding desired results. It lacked something and somewhere. Perhaps they did not follow the prescribed formula in their rituals properly. The priest or *pandit* adds such type of negative feelings in their mind-set. Sometimes, Pandit says you may not choose the right time, date and place at the time of performing rituals as I suggested. This process continues like this way. People usually have failed to come out of it in their whole life. They even join their relatives in this process.

Black Magic

Pandits force them to believe in such type of process. Priests, astrologers, half-baked physicians and 'black magic' are the main guider to run their fate or business successfully. They in fact also sometime mislead by the so-called society. They want to come out of it but the vicious circle of astrological marketing is so strong that people remain trapped. They are bound to follow them blindly. They lose their self-confidence and respect. They even sacrifice someone's child to have his own child. They won't mind doing any evil practice for the sake of their own benefit.

Today, we find all TV channels are giving space to these astrologers. They spent large money for the publicity. Obviously, they will recover their huge spending in publicity in double way from the innocent people which eventually go to the TV channels. It is a big business. It is sad that the intellectual and educated people of the society and even the government also are not paying their due attention to save the innocents and deptressed from their gripss. They watch this game silently and laughed at such type of practice. TV channels say they show different kinds of programmes. It is up to the people what they want to see. One wonders, why it is not checked. It is really shocking.

Laxmi Yantra

Our popular film actors also appear in these advertisements to attract the innocents. One sells a Mahalaxmi *Yantra*. The other sells some other token of superstitions. Their aim is to trap people. For example, one Vinod Chourasia says, he had a four by four feet pan shop. This Laxmi *yantra* changed his destiny. Today he has a flourishing business in crores. Imagine, anyone will be enticed toward it but actually if it worked like this way then everyone would have become millionaires like Chourasia. In fact, in reality such Laxmi *yantras* don't change anyone's life and fate. How can an alien Laxmi *yantra* change your life? Understand one thing no one will come to change your life. Nothing is going to happen suddenly. Your life will become the way you will plan it and it depends on your understanding and thinking. The way you perceive and act on it, success will be yours and that will be permanent. The ordinary people don't understand this game and they wait to see change in their future on the basis of predictions. May be a lottery will change their future. They believe in the reports of the newspapers, who tell them that their life is going to change. It is really painful, even after doing all this one is not get success and get also disappointed. One thing is certain that the successful people reached wherever they are because of their positive thinking, effort and knowledge. Nothing is more pious then knowledge. People are rich and happy because of knowledge. People don't understand such a small thing. These superstitious create false thinking in people's mind. They start believing that they will be soon very rich. Positive predictions may not come true but negatives turn out to be effective and true. One becomes a victim of frustration and disappointments in life.

The fact is that many children are born in the same time. It means their future according to star should be similar but it doesn't happen. If their stars are same why their life is not similar? Why the life of twins is not similar? People even try to rectify the stars positions of their children. They even delay the birth of their child after consulting these astrologers. They go for the next child according to auspicious time. Thinking that despite doing all this, nothing changes. Life goes on despite all these factors. They keep repeating the same life-style and rituals that they have been performing for many years and can not make use of their knowledge and experience to get results.

Destiny Comes From Thought

People should listen to their soul and instead of following these superstitious notions. Know yourself. Find your interest and ability and work accordingly. It should be understood. First comes the idea and after accepting it, idea leads to action. Then it will repeat and become your habit. It is a known fact that your habits become your personality. Your personality becomes your destiny. So what we are trying to say here is your destiny comes from your thought not from astrology, sun sign, stars and numerology. The people who believe in these negative thoughts can not achieve anything in life. You have to bring purity, sincerity and honesty in your thoughts and actions.

Take the case of an alcoholic. He must come from a background where this is quite common. This interest must have had an origin. Now, he is an addict because he gets it from his environment. He has been drinking for years. Suppose he changes his environment. In the new setting no one drinks. He thinks why so? He gets an idea. It is bad. He stops drinking. The astrologers play the same game. They influence people's mind without any bases and run their business. They attack your thought process and misguide you to lead a fearful life. They suggest you the all sorts of strange ideas about performing rituals and ask you to wear ruby, diamond, various stones according to their understanding. And you get influence by them and do whatever they suggest whether it is expensive means or the harmful way of doing things.

Karwa-chouth

Women are an easy prey of these astrologers. They should be made aware of this. They believe more than men but nothing changes. Their men folk spend a lot of money but nothing happens. There is total loss. Why they are doing it? Why women get attracted more easily. In fact, the ball comes back to marketing of God and the accessories. Women follow a kind of rat-race. They compete with each other. *Karwa-chouth* is the most saleable product. Rich and famous sell it. It has acquired an international acceptance. Have you met anybody who got benefitted by *Karwa-chouth.* Did they achieve anything in life or interpersonal relations or character building? Nothing is reported on this in TV channels and newspapers. No one talks about the loss incurred.

We are keeping this *Karwa-chouth* fast for centuries without knowing its good and bad effects. Have you ever thought how a poor people arrange money and do other formalities for this occasion? It is displaying only a ritual and creating wrong nuances among female that on this particular day they can demand anything to her husband. Later on, female compare their gifts with their friends and colleagues. Now, the point is this *Karwa-chouth* fast is adding any value in their life. If you observe this closely that has got no meaning and objective.

Fasting came in our life to keep us healthy. Today women eat more when, they break the fast. It has become a fashion. *Karwa-chouth* talks the billing. The priests have even worked on husbands to keep it. It has become a big drama. TV channels also join the race. Not all women but about 70 per cent worship their husband this day but their behaviour is same sarcastic and demanding. This is a symbol of an undefined relationship. Why to create a drama out of it? The filthy rich even gift a crore or two on these occasions. The lesser beings feel jilted.

To create more and more superstitious, well-known and respectable personalities, achievers, women politicians and film stars ostentatiously display this *Karwa-chouth* ritual to influence masses. They try to set an example among masses to perform this ritual in grand way. Even they do not understand the benefit of this ritual. Nobody has got any specific benefit out of it rather lost freedom to get rid of this type of ritual that also destroys the inter-personal relation. It is performed by leading personalities of repute in the society. General people follow these kinds of rituals blindly and keep performing without giving any thought to it. They lack objectivity, creativity and innovation in their work and purpose.

A poet has said *Ek shanshah ne banwa ke tajmahal hum garibon ki muhabbat ka udaya hai mazak.*

There is something disturbing about *Karwa-chouth.* It should stop. It sends a wrong message to the society. People compete among each other. It affects human relationship. How can you judge a relation with money? It has no business to continue. But no one wants to stop it. The priest astrologers and the market all are gainers.

These people damage the society. Sacrificing innocent kids, superstitions over spending and exploitation of women. Such exploitations have appeared in newspapers. They brain wash women. Talk about past life. Claim their long relationships through different births. In last carnation you were my wife. They made innocent women to surrender. Why? How does it benefit anybody?

Only weak people follow these fast. They have less money. Not a stable mind. They always have wavering mind and no clarity in their action and thought. They lack everything in their personality. Hence, get exploited by *Pandits* and *Pujaris*. They want to remain like that taking it as their destiny.

Clouded Vision

Man is the best divine creation. Man is not meant to be exploited. The reason behind it the people are fearful and have undesirable demands prone to get exploited. They are not in a position to face real facts of life. Listen to your soul and follow it. It will change your state and direction. You are the property of the soul. You are alive till the time soul exists in you otherwise your body is without soul you are lifeless. Everyman has different problem and opportunities then why to copy others. You have to apply your original thought, idea and action.

Those who visit temple and mosque tie a secret string. One ties it the other opens it. Life goes on like that. You offer sweets. You might find it being sold after sometime. It happens with every offering. We notice such action but never oppose them. We don't want to oppose any faith. We don't want to create any issue out of it. Oppose it, suppose a rich and famous contribute to its continuation. The rich and famous personalities influence and exploit common people to support the religious organisations. You and I don't realise this game. Only a part comes in front of us. Who knows the reality behind this religious game? Who paid how much to whom to attract and influence masses? But people tend to believe that if you donate like the rich and famous you will also become rich and famous. This is marketing.

This way, common people want to follow rich and famous people's activities, without understanding its pros and cons. You get hypnotised to the rich and famous. You think that you will also become like them as they become rich and famous. You forget to have that kind of status, life style and become rich and famous, you have to inculcate, purity, wisdom, liberty, real devotion, principles within you, plus you have to forcefully clear the delusion of sinful clouded eyes.

Those who visit religious places they also know that how much thought and disciplined character went in to their present success. How they acquired new perspective and practiced the acquisition of knowledge. They concentrated more to adopt divine character and their profession. They deliberately avoid it cheap entertainment which could have led them to a wrong path. In order to be a successful and create an identity in the society, they had to focus their concentration to sustain their achievement in the long run. It would not have been possible by mere visiting the temples and mosques. It is easy to go to a temple many people do that but can they claim any big success which has a public profile. It is absolutely clear like a mirror image that the human achievements are not possible by rituals. One doesn't get success easily. If visiting temples would have brought salvation then there would have been a large number of successful people in the country. But today we can count such people on our finger tips. By inviting a star to a religious place we try to make it popular. It is a powerful marketing of these religious places but a common man can't understand and see through it. In fact, the popularity of a religious place is not because of their factual benefit to the masses. It is because of professional sublime creative marketing approaches that have been adopted by the trusties of such religious places.

Pretend to be Religious

People pretend to be religious, by doing so they want to create a following. They become popular. They appear on poster and banners. They organise *Sai-Sandhya, Jagrata,* and *Mata-ki-Chouki* to appease gods and goddesses. But whosoever attends these religious functions are not aware about the real objective of *Jagrata* to aware and get enlightened from within. They think their physical presence and sleepless night, have tea and coffee together, pass time with liquor and drugs are the real objectives of these kind of social gathering. The one who organise and contribute in *Jagrata* fund their objectives are clear that people should treate them religious and God-fearing person. By doing this, they open new avenues for themselves and create a platform to do business with people and expand their family relations.

A poet has said :

Aaj jo jitna sammanit hai wo utna hi shaq ke dayre mein hai means one who is as much respected is in doubts in same measure.

We want to know from you. The God will not provide you everything if you do not work devotedly with full awareness and with a bit of innovation in your work. In fact, people got trapped by such action. The same TV channels have reported them. Be it *mahakumbh* of Allahabad, an accident in Himachal temple or pilgrims of Kedarnath. People follow any popular action. They act without realising the outcome. They even take small kids, women and elderly people. Little realising that there can be chaos. There can a bomb blast, it is collective madness. Not a few but millions join the mad race. People enjoy being a part of a crowd. He gets something to talk rest of his life. How glorious was the temple, the food, the arrangement and the cold water. This collective madness is the product of marketing. You become a part of it but soon return to the same anger, jealousy and the fraud which you were doing earlier. Why is this? This gets a label of being religious.

It is not that people don't get shocked. They get it regularly but they don't change. Man learns by serious problems but only if he doesn't lose his self-confidence. He has to make constant efforts. He had to accept the challenges. All of us get such challenges very few accept them others don't. You don't reach anywhere. If you will accept challenges you should not be disturbed by problems, in fact problems lead to growth and it is an eye opener for you. You can realise your shortcomings clearly.

Kawaria

You must have observed for the last one decade the *Kawaria's* are very much into fashion. According to people's believe, they travel bare foot to go to *Gangotry,* that is origin of river Ganges and bring holy water to their area and pour it on Lord Shiva's *Shiv-linga*'s. We see many unemployed youth take part in this act. The interesting thing is number of these youths are increasing every years in *kawaria's karvan.* In the month of august that is considered to be the month of Lord Shiva according to Hindu mythology, we find that roads are jam everywhere, *kawarias* dance on road on high volume music, one can see *kawaria* dance on running truck in busy road, they have got *Danda* and *lathi* (Stick) in their hand, if a pedestrian and office-goer or common man will dare to object about their collective mass madness, they have got every right beating to him up right there. Because of these religious processions working people face lots of difficulties on road while going and returning from their offices. Local politicians make arrangements for these *Kawarias* on roads, Central government and State government give them full security, and sometimes they divert traffic because of these processions. *Kawaria's* enjoy their entire journey and return with holy water to their respective areas. Then the villagers worship them as if they are the ancestors of Lord Shiva. It sum up with pouring water on Lord Shiva and later followed by V*andara,* the feast for the common people. Do they get any real benefit that they are free from anger, jealousy, greed, cruelty for better life to be better human being?

Don't you think it is madness of people? Just because of, they do not have anything to do meaningful in their life they become a part of this maddening crowd. Are they really achieving something by doing all this? Why local politicians are supporting these kinds of processions? Why the government is supporting these processions? Are we ready if there will be religious riots? What is the aim and objective of these *Kawaria's?* If you say to find Lord Shiva or to please Lord Shiva then they should understand the almighty God is everywhere. You need not to go anywhere. It is within you. There are lots of questions like are they getting any benefit out of it? Is it helping them in shaping their future? Is this the kind of nation we are looking for where the youth is misguided by our politicians and government? Why these TV channels are silent on this? Why the whole media is silent that is considered to be the fourth pillar of democracy? We strongly think that we need to introspect and use this youth's energy in nation-building activities.

Keep Faith in God

Real believers need not go to a temple. God has created everything inside you. Just look unto yourself. Some argue the pilgrimage includes tourism. This is a dangerous proposition. God is not a light phenomenon. It has its own power. If you want to be a tourist be one but not by insulting the God. If you believe and accept the God's is omnipresent and omnipotent then why you go out to reach him. It means you are contradicting your thoughts and beliefs.

No one is happy with this present condition. You think tomorrow will be golden. You dreams for better future but you forgets that his future depends on presently what is good you are doing with pure thinking. If you can't face the present boldly nothing new will happen in your future. Man generally cribs. Keep on cribbing. Nothing is permanent in this world. If you want you can change the present in any manner. If you will be meaningful the change will be same. If you will work aimlessly everything will become aimless. It is to be understood. Have a deeper look at your life. Try to understand the society. Look into all spiritual action from whom they have benefitted. If you will accept challenges in your life then only you can improve your life. Everything is hidden in these propositions. The answer is, you didn't want to accept any challenges.

Your belief in God is merely an escape from your monotonous, stupid and cruel life.

-Jiddu Krishnamurthi

If the educated women knew that nothing has changed in their life by practicing rituals like fasting then they should leave this hypocrisy. If illiterate women also did not get any benefit by these rituals then they should resort to educating themselves. They should leave aside all hesitations to move ahead in life. Even if it means, making their children as the tutors. If they have got married to an educated man then they should study through him. If their family doesn't have an educated person then they should go to a tutor. They should get knowledge through books. We have emphasised many a times that nothing is more pious then knowledge in this world. As you can't see anything clear in a dark closed room similarly illiteracy and ignorance don't lead to progressive joyful life.

Therefore, such people have to bear poverty and ignorance throughout their life. Again the solution lies in making a friendly relationship with the soul. You should listen to its voice. It is desirable to follow the voice of inner-soul. They should integrate in the life. They should follow such a path this is the only path of truth. If you follow the truth your self-confidence will multiply many a times you will get answers to your questions. Try to understand it by assuming that everybody is taking an examination in the world. All of them have different question papers but in the school of life the answers of everybody are same. As we follow them blindly without using our intellect and experience.

If you follow the path shown by the soul you will become bold. Whenever you will face massive problems then instead of going to a Temple, Mosques or Gurudwara you will look your inner-self to form a close relationship by the divine part of your soul. This way you will be anchor of your own life. That way you will be able to do all that which you wanted to do in life and still are interested in it. You will have to introspect and find the answer of this question that if somebody else can be successful then why not you. You should respect and trust yourself. You have all the elements to succeed. You just have to recognise the proper talent and interest in your profession.

8

Money and Other Riches

Enormity of Wealth

Have you ever noticed that there is wealth spread all over in the vicinity of the nature? We never find poverty in nature's conduct. Look minutely at the nature around us to find that the God has given us so many mountains but we can't visit them in a life time. There is so much of water on earth that you can't consume. The sky over our head is so large that you can't cover it. There is an abundance of jungle you can't enjoy them all. The flowers are so beautiful that you will get exhausted by looking at them. There are so many fruits that you can't eat them all. You can't finish the whole food. We want to say that there is enormity of wealth everywhere. There is no trace of poverty in nature.

God for instance and you won't find him lacking in any field. Man is the best creation of God. He has made you competent and affluent from every point of view. Let's begin with man's mind. We can use only a small part of it. The surveys tell us that today an average man uses only three to four per cent of his mind. Extraordinary people use 10 per cent of it. The rest 90 per cent remain unutilised the whole life.

You can't say that the God has left anything incomplete. Despite this why a man is poor. It is an important question that wealth which he has gathered by hook and crook he considers it as its riches but it in fact it is not riches. We may tell you that the wealth of money is the wealth of the lowest category. If you have money that doesn't mean that you are rich. Today wherever you look you will find a race to become rich. Everybody wants to earn more and more money. You are craving for money, oh money, oh God money. Almost everybody is mad after money. He is becoming crazy for money. Everybody wants money. If he has some money, he wants more. If he earns more money he still wants more how much money a man needs. There is no limit in his mind. All around there seems to be an environment of loot. Money is desired at any cost. Whatever may have to be done to earn more money if you look at worldly life you will find that person who has unlimited money, he is more unhappy.

Unlimited Money

For example, just presume one Mr Arora accepted money as God in his life. Today he has abundant money in all the banks of the country. He is not able to control his money which is there in his foreign bank account. He has all kinds of property which he has earned by using all the unfair and foul means. He has three sons beside his wife in his family. His sons are fighting over money and property. His wife is deeply pained. Mr Arora is deeply a frustrated person and at the last phase of his life he was in pain. He is totally disturbed mentally. He is sick. Mr Arora spends more time in hospitals. His wife is also in the hospital almost half of her time. None of Mr Arora's sons visit him. His sons do not have time to talk to him. If they meet him then it is either to get some papers signed or to discuss the issues of money and property. Nobody has time to look after him. It is a big matter for his sons that their father is being treated in a well-known hospital in the country. All the sons pretend to be busy. Mrs Arora had seen in life how her husband was running after money. Mr Arora never listened to her advice. Money was everything for him in life. Money was a mother, father, brother, sister or even a wife for him. Everything was money. His wife suffered a lot in his craving to earn more money. Since her children were small she could not leave him. She had hoped that perhaps when her children will mature they would understand her better. Today all her hopes have broken. She is sad. Mr Arora while lying in the hospital bed keeps on thinking where things went wrong.

Today 95 per cent people with money are in the same condition. You must have understood that why we were saying that the riches of money are the richness of the lowest category. You are rich but only because of money. But what to do with that money which can't let you have two moments alone for you. There is no mutual love. It is not a family. Just think what such a family can give to society and community? This family is scared of its pains and agony. What support that family can give to others who are helpless? This story of Mr Arora is the story of millions of people.

Richness of Knowledge

Now, we come to the real issue. In fact, people like Mr Arora are unable to understand while racing for money that what they are doing? They want to earn so much that their seven generations sit and eat and still they will have money. Is there anything apart from money that they should care for instead of their wealth which they are taking so importantly? In fact, the richness of money has nothing big about it. One should be rich by knowledge, good character, self-respect, good health, richness of relations and richness of values. Let's understand this richness one by one as why we are saying it like that. You might be finding it strange but we want to place the truth in front of you.

First of all, we take the richness of knowledge. If the God has given you such a beautiful body, heart and mind then why don't you use it properly? It is a big question that everybody should ask from himself. If you will acquire knowledge, read good books then you will be able to differentiate between what is good and what is bad. By these ideas you will be able to benefit yourself but even your family and society. Only knowledge is valuable in the world. You have made a firm resolution. You have to remind yourself about this resolution every day. Only then your resolution will be firm. You don't have to get your knowledge dusted. You have to polish, refine and update it regularly. All those big jobs that have been possible because of the knowledge are not hidden from anyone. There are many examples in the world where many people were born in extreme poverty and they were immensely successful. This miracle happened because they recognised their ability. They brightened it by the light of knowledge. They did not let it dust gather on that knowledge and they produced a wonder in the world. That man who has found divine knowledge only he has touched the sky heights. This is also so that you could not have got that divine knowledge without listening to the voice of your soul. If you will take decisions in your life according to the voice of your soul then no one can stop you from being successful in life. You will progress every day. You should identify your interest, the tilt of your mind and your nature. What you are firm on, you have to act after recognising it and according to your ability. You might fall short of money in your life but you would not feel the ability to work on your resolution and you would even take the lack of money as a challenge and develop your brain to solve this shortcoming by acquiring knowledge regularly.

You will gain all kinds of happiness. Now, you decide for yourself that what kind of richness you want.

Richness of Character

If you have the richness of character there can't be anything better than that. If you listen to your inner-soul then you can't do anything wrong by listening to this voice. You will be able to avoid all kind of evils. You will not indulge in bad habits like liquor, cigarette, illegal sex, fraud, greed, craving and jealousy in your character. Your circle will invite good people. You will earn credibility in the society. People will take you as worthy of trust. People will take your word as reliable. You will immensely progress in your business. Now you tell yourself that if a man has richness of knowledge and character than who would not like to get connected to such a people? Will he lack anything? Is this richness not bigger than the meager riches of money?

Now you would have understood that why did we call the riches of money as of the lowest category of riches. Apart from the richness of knowledge and character, the man has another big wealth. He is generally not aware of this richness. This richness is off his self-respect. You must have heard about being integrity in life. This richness of self-respect and integrity in reality teaches the purpose to live. The man who does not have self-respect cannot do anything good or big in life. All the great people had a common quality. They all were immensely self-respecting and sensitive. It gave them a unique character. They achieved a lot of success in life but they never took anything which didn't belong to them. This quality of character made them a different person. When you don't grab someone else's right then you have to be competent in your own field. This is compulsory for you. We mean that you have to be best in your field. If you adopt this quality then you will leave behind all negativity. The character of self-respect is a unique quality. Today it appears that such people have been lost in pages of history. It is not completely true that such people do not exist in this world. There are many people in this world whose character is there greatest capital. This very self-respecting quality has inspired them to do great feats in the world. Just think the self-respecting character and richness is a biggest asset. One whose nature is self-respecting and has integrity might lack money in life but he would not lack the profile of a man with integrity. Integrity keeps a man in his limit. Right from the beginning, it doesn't' need to show off. This is certain that one get destroyed by showing off.

Richness of Relationship

The richness of relationships and values is not less than any other wealth. Allow us to explain the depth of human relation by an example. Suppose somebody invited you to his house. You live in Delhi and he who called you who lives in Mumbai. When you reached Mumbai, he came to airport to receive you. He took you to his house in his car. He treated you very nicely. He left nothing in his hospitality. He came to airport to see you off. Next time when he came to Delhi you didn't have a car therefore he had to come on his own to your house. You welcomed him. When he reached your house whatever was availabl ' it was offered to him. You too spend some time together and he left for Mumbai.

After three months you went to Mumbai to meet him. This time he neither came to receive you at the airport nor played a host like the last time. He didn't come to airport to see you off. What will you say at this situation? Some people might readily comment that it had to happen. Because the world is like that, in our opinion the Mumbai gentleman used the power in a wrong way. He had the means to do what he did but he did not do it. You did not have those facilities therefore. You did what you could. But he did not behave the way he did earlier. This is dishonesty. This is dishonesty in relationship. This is a wealth of relationship. It has to be understood minutely.

If you are transparent in your relationships then you should give them importance. You should not behave in a petty manner. You should respect your relations. Then what is that which you can't achieve. When we are born on this earth then we inherit some relationship like parents, brother and sister, etc., apart from these relationship whatever we form that is according to our thinking. It is because of our good behaviour. These very good relationships later become our strength. They help us a lot to attain heights in life. Just think what else can be richer than cordial relation only that person can preserve his relation who is aware of the soul. What else is better than the knowledge of soul? What is an evil? It is necessary to understand this. Success lies in this understanding.

Health is Wealth

After the richness of relationship in life we shall talk about the wealth of values. If the values of your present and past life are good then you are an owner of great wealth. If you conserve this you can progress by following a value based life and progress a lot. Good values mean those characteristics which you inherit in your childhood. It includes respect to parents, consideration to elders, following the truth, avoiding fraud and wrong behaviour refrain from killing any living being and similar qualities. When people will see such good qualities in you, they would like to get connected. You will be rolling in money but if your values are corrupt then what respect can you earn in society. You can with hold this wealth of values also by the knowledge of soul. If you are close to your soul then you will never let your high values get corrupted and you will retain this wealth for all times to come.

Let's talk a little about the wealth of health. If you have good health, then take it from us that no one is richer than you. We gave you an example of Mr Arora. Just think there was no shortage of money, God had given him a good wife, three sons but an unhealthy body. Let's go back to the initial phase of his life. When Mr Arora must have been a healthy person we would like to clear a point here that the God did not send a sick Mr Arora to this world. God does not send indisposed people to this world. You invite sickness yourself in your body and sick body is an apt example of your dishonesty in your conduct and behaviour. You were not fair in your dealing with the people. Your sickness is the result of that. Your body invites diseases every day. Your fair and foul behaviour with people, wrong food habits, toxic, negative and revengeful thoughts, polluted environment and money earned by wrong means. How can our poor and inferior body can bear these poisonous attacks?

Uncontrolled Desires

That is why people suffer with sickness and remain unhappy in life. People don't have control on their desires. They don't care for the quality of food. First they eat without bothering its quality. Then they spend money on getting treated. It happens because they do not have elementary knowledge about proper food. There is saying in Punjabi.

"bhukya bhookh na utre, je khaven lakh bar"

It means the hungry doesn't feel satisfied even by eating one lakh time and again. His belly becomes full but his jealousy and desire of his eyes for food are not satisfied and he remains trapped.

Mr Arora also became sick because of his faulty conduct and corrupt nature. His food habits were careless. He was greedy and fraudulent as well as his intension were wrong that is why he became sick. Why does it happen? Let's understand this also. When you are behaving unfairly then your wrong actions burden your mind and body constantly. Soul gets weak. It affects your body also. It puts your life in danger. You start doubting people. You don't get a sound sleep in the night. This trend continues for years. Imagine how unfair with your body. Today Mr Arora has limitless money. He has large possessions of gold and silver despite the amount of property the truth is that his body is suffering from all kinds of sickness.

"It is health that is real wealth and not pieces of gold and silver"

—M.K. Gandhi

An insecurity, fear, disappointment, frustration, complex, inferiority, deeply pained heart rejection by your own people, regret, insult and loneliness have already killed you even if your body is alive with the help of medicines. Just think if Mr Arora had heard the voice of his soul and acted accordingly then how his life would have been? You must have got the answer. If a man has a healthy body then everything will be in place because a healthy mind and brain develop only in a healthy body. It is well-known that you can't buy good health with money but if you are hail and hearty then you can earn money. You have to do *yoga* everyday for good health. Such a man can be completely pedantic and proper by keeping his dealings correct and with his pleasure. It will be the first dose to a sick man. Doctors can treat him well if his mental behaviour is also correct. It is necessary to live a discipline life such a man will not feel the shortage of funds. Can richness of money is bigger than good health. Now, you must have understood it well that why the wealth of money falls lowest among riches. Every person needs money but only that much with which he can look after his family comfortably. He has a house to live in. Here a question arise what other utility money could have? Why people need money after their needs are fulfilled.

People have other priorities in life that is why they chase money day in and day out. They need money to maintain a particular standard. You will find people saying that their son studies in that well-known school. They have a trendy and expensive car. It is chauffer driven car. They have many servants at home. They boost that they wear only branded cloths. Our son is always in air-conditioned surrounding. His school is air condition. Our house is centrally air conditioned. We even spend Rs 50 lakh rupee on *Jagrata* every year. We have spent Rs two crores each on the marriage of every child. When people behave like this their children also get affected. Whatever example we have given there is not one which is compulsory for anyone. When people talk like this they try to copy others. They also want to be like that. Is this the only yardstick to live in the society? Can they live in peace after doing all this? There show off behaviour sends a wrong massage in the society. Because of these useless actions, jealousy is on the rise in the society. No one is happy with each other. Our society is struggling with this serious problem. We feel by now. You must have fully understood the real meaning of being rich.

9

The Path to Soul is Real Path to Success

Success in Life

Who doesn't want success in life? Who doesn't like to be successful? Who doesn't want that success should follow him? At least once in a life time, you want to have a taste of success. But if success was possible only because you wanted it, it would have been easy for us to get successful. People pray to God, offer various things in order to get achievement. Have you ever thought about those people who have got success in life? Are you really worthy of getting successful? Let's introspect and see whether you have the qualities of being successful. You will also discuss on the qualities that are required to achieve greater heights.

In the last chapters, you learned how you can know your soul and how you can develop a good relationship with it. Soul is the eternal truth. Without knowing soul, nothing is possible. Who all have been successful in life, knew the essence of life—soul. This knowledge you got from your family values and the knowledge you acquired after knowing soul. This is just like opening the doors of heaven. People, who know the soul, know the world. These people have done big things in life and given innovations to this world. These people have something in common. They are mostly found with lot of self-respect. This is the main quality found in these people. If somebody has this, you can think you have it all to become big in life. All he needs is honesty and loyalty. You have to balance all these and you will be a complete man.

High Self-esteem

Let us discuss this in detail. If you know somebody has lot of self- respect, you talk about him with respect automatically. You know that he is dignified and carries himself well. People might not agree with him all the time in public, but they know what he is saying is right. He will not change his principles for anything. He is decent and determined. People with high self-esteem, do not bother what other people think about them.

If you look around, you find successful people have lot of integrity in them. Of all the people that are working in this world, either they have integrity or disloyalty in their nature. There is third category also some people are in between, means they depend on others like parasites. You must notice that many business families had to close down their business. Some of them are literally on the road. Why it happened there must be some reasons behind it. Because after a point they had not listened to their soul and got failed. No success is permanent in this world. If you are successful it doesn't mean that you should stop to hear your inner-soul. It means God has assigned you to achieve some bigger goal.

When we talk about people, who are not committed or disloyal, we mean people who are implementing all kinds of ways to do their work. These kinds of people will do anything for their benefit. They deceive society, and government everybody and they are very harmful for the world at large. These people rather than reducing are increasing in numbers day by day.

Now, there are people who have lot of integrity and these people are very few in the society. But these are the people who have done big works in the world. It is only self-respect and decency, which takes a person to greater heights. It is only this quality of loyalty that people are able to make it big. It cannot happen without your soul's consent. Your soul keeps telling you what to do and what not to do. If you listen to it, you can never go wrong. People who go according to their soul give a direction to the world also.

Sensitivity

How can we see the person with integrity and self-respect? Let's discuss this with a fitting incident. Once upon a time, there was a big thief. He used to rob all affluent people in the city. If he robbed somebody, that particular person used to get famous. People thought if there is a robbery in someone's place, he must be very rich. Otherwise, why will this thief rob him? So you can imagine how smart, clever and popular this thief was? Once he got fed-up of stealing, he came to his *guru*. He told his problem to *guru* Nagarjuna that he does not want to rob people anymore. He wants to leave robbery. *Guru* simply said, "What is there to think. Stop stealing". Thief said, if it was that easy, why would have I come to you? Guru said,– Ok, next time, when you go to steal somebody and the moment you raise your hand to steal the actual object, then stop for a moment and ask yourself,- is this yours? Thief listened to this carefully and went away. Next time, when he was about to steal and pick up gold and jewelleries, he asked himself—is this mine? The answer was "no". After that he went to many places. But the answer was no. He came back home and had a sound sleep that night. In the morning, he got up fresh. He had got rid of his bad habit of stealing forever. This type of sleep he never enjoyed in his full life as per his memory goes.

We would like to say that all these people, who are very good or big or are dacoits and robbers, are very sensitive too, inside. They do things extraordinarily, so they are not mediocre, e.g., are Tulsidas, Valmiki, Anguliman, John Milton, Mahatma Gandhi, Mahatma Budha, Thomas Alva Edison etc...

They think that we should not take anything what is not ours. This is self-respect and integrity. These people will have so many other qualities also. He always achieves success in life. He has lot of loyalty and honesty. He will give everybody their credit. He will never take what is not his. He has lot of self-confidence. Nobody can sway him from his principles. This type of person is very good for society and behaves also responsible way. He just does what he thinks is right. He doesn't believe in pseudo values of society. He doesn't promise anything false to anybody. He just listens to his voice of inner-soul and believes in God.

Self-motivation

There is a very good quality in these kinds of people. That is self- motivation. These people don't need any push. They work themselves. This is a very important quality in them. These people are perfectionist. They work and devote time and money to create extraordinary projects only. They want everything perfect. They work with complete dedication and don't bow down in front of anybody. They are self-sacrificing by nature. They do not get into bad habits and keep themselves away from all bad things and practices.

This type of person has no show off tendencies. He doesn't get into false boasting and bragging about himself. He just keeps focus on his work. He gives people their due credit, respects and others talent. He is a leader and blessed with divine power. He is calm, composed, disciplined, and honest and at the same time he appreciates others good qualities.

Dignified person is not scared of anybody. He is brave and can take on challenges. He has an ability to take risk. No work is big without challenges. All success in this world has been achieved when people have taken risk and faced challenges. He has boldly faced challenges and got victory. Let's tell you the story of Sikander.

Jo Jeeta Wahi Sikander

When Sikander thought of conquering the world, he had to enter India through the way of Afganistan. When he told his army to cross Jhelum river his army got scared seeing so many crocodiles in the water. They refused to go. When Sikander saw this, he jumped into the river and started fighting those crocodiles with his sword. Seeing his master's courage army got very encouraged and also jumped into the water. They cleared all the crocodiles with bravery and crossed the river in short span of time. That is why we say— *"jo jeeta wahi sikander"*. He was undefeated in battle and is considered one of history's most successful commanders. People can become Sikander only if they show this bravery and courage. Not all can become Sikander. Integrated, dignified people go a long way. They read books, they travel, do self-introspection, and on the basis of their talent they do new innovation and discoveries by finding plus and minus characters in them.

These people focus on only one work. They don't run after 10 things. They are not fickle minded. They work with full-dedication and honesty. They always try to achieve their aim and put their best to get it. These kinds of people deserve to get big success in life. They don't cheat people and do their work with full dedication and concentration. Who doesn't remember the great archer Arjuna in *Mahabharata.* He was an extraordinary archer and was so good that he could shoot at the moving in circles fish's eye even while seeing its image in water. Is it easy?

It was an extraordinary task. That is why *Veer* Arjuna was considered as the finest archer and a peerless warrior by many notable figures in the *Mahabharata* and the history will remember him for ages.

We also see that people in general do not support people with integrity and decency. They love him in private but do not support him publically. People are generally scared from society and weak in nature. They think these straight forward people are a big threat to this disorganised system. They are comfortable with today's chaos. Generally, people are insecure and they label these people as adamant and selfish.

Dignified People

People with integrity accept their mistakes. One who has the courage to accept his mistakes is a matured and dignified person. You need a lot of courage to accept your mistake. If you cannot accept your mistake it means you cannot exploit your future. One should not have false ego. Dignified people think positive and respect others. Achieve big success and are progressive in their approach.

Dignified people are sensitive also. They see the pain of others. Sometimes, they are too sensitive about themselves also. They also have good health and a charm on their face. Their every action is dedicated to humanity. They ought to have good health because of their disciplined nature and that is his birth-right. This is the proof and result of his honest behaviour and dealing with people.

People who have integrity are healthy, keeps high values and they are pillar of strength in their family. These are the parameter of success. The families who are deprived from these values have got rift among them. On the other hand, the family who has got peace and prosperity due to all these virtues integrated in their family and characters. All the family members live together happily and make progress also in a loving way.

Now, you can well understand how important it is to be dignified and integrated. These people have courage to take on any kind of work and challenges and they are not scared of facing any difficulties. They guide others and always ready to extend their help in the development of a good society. They are the leaders. One who can lead with focus, dedication, honesty, only he can achieve big success in life and can also set a precedent for others in the society.

10

God Makes us with What We Offer Him

10

God Makes us with What We Offer Him

God is Great Creator

In previous chapters, we have amply emphasised that man is the best and wonderful creation of God. It is a unique creation of the supreme divine power. He has not made any human being weak. When we make a product in our day to day life then how happy we are. We take it to the market to multiply our profit. The product is same but we make its copies and keep on selling it. The God has not created any duplicate. Every human being is original, unique and distinct. In this world, every person is different from each other in looks behaviour and habits. We mean to say the God has created every human being different. How great creator is God that he has the skill and power to create a man. Today a man may progress immensely but he has not been able to produce even human blood. The man is distinguished on this earth. It means you are distinguished in the eyes of the God. As you have to trust your product because otherwise you will not be able to create a demand for it. Similarly, you will have to trust the body provided by the God. You will have to respect it. Today if you look around we will find that man doesn't trust himself. He doesn't know why he has come on this earth? The whole life of people is spent in eating, fighting, greediness, jealousy, deceiving, sex and taking revenge. Living in the same house, people live different life. In the same house, someone lives in a haven and another in hell. Have you ever thought, why? For example, there is a family of four members. Father, mother and two children, elder one is daughter and younger one is son. All have born on this earth. You generally find that all have different nature, taste, behaviours and habits. Why is that so? Because, when you take rebirth, they carry their last birth account also. This family is also carrying their last account but all have different accounts but the God have chosen to live them together. All of them are different soul with their *karmic* account. That is why we find someone is always contented and happy in every situation, but at the same house we find other one is aggressive and agitated all the time. So, it is in most of the family. We live with different soul in same house but someone lives in heaven and other one lives in hell.

Karmic Accounts

Let us look at it and discuss minutely to understand it in a better way. Any human being, who is born on this earth, comes here with the actions done in his previous berth. He not only completes the actions started in previous life but also does all fair and foul actions. He doesn't stop even for a moment to think what he is doing? Now, presume as an example in past life. When you took birth on this earth then you are expected to complete those actions which you had left half-way. Now, you have got an opportunity that you complete them in this life. They are called your *karmic* accounts. You are born again and again to settle your *Karmic* accounts. Understand that if a child fails repeatedly in tenth class then will he gets admission in 11th class? When he will pass in 10th only then he will study in 11th class. The man also fails again and again in the cycle of life and is reborn in the next life with his *karmic* accounts.

We had just mentioned that in the same house one lives in heaven and another in hell. What we mean to say that if you can improve your personality by recognising your *karmic* account, if you make a new resolution everyday and improve your habits. If you follow truth in life and bring self-respect in your life and eventually hear the voice of your inner-soul then you are living in heaven. Take another picture. You are born in a family with your *karmic* account. You already have some old account from your previous berth and top of it you deal with people in a wrong manner. You live a life of greed, fraud and dishonesty. In such a situation, you are living in hell. Such people are restless, disturbed, frustrated, disappointed leading to a sick body and living with pain and agony. Let's try to understand that how this *karmic* account comes in your life. When you lead the life of falsehood, fraud and dishonesty then all wrong feelings are born in your mind and brain as jealousy, greed, bad intention, cruelty and ruthlessness are created, they become a part of your life. This might appear awkward that God makes us with that material which we provide him. If we are giving such a matter then he will create us with this same material. When you produce a product then it turns out according to the raw material. Let's ask you, can you produce the best quality of product by using inferior raw material? You will get the answer yourself. The God will make you according to the raw material we will provide him. As two lawyers argue the case of an accused by giving different examples though the law is same. If the accused has not committed a murder then what will be the verdict of judge. The judge has nothing in his hand. If the accused has committed murder then he will be punished and if he has not committed the murder then he will not get the punishment. The role of the judge is dependant on fact and proofs. The judge can give his verdict only on the basis of given facts and proofs by the lawyers. He has to understand and give the verdict according to the circumstances and the facts provided. The judge can't act on his own even if he desires. He has to call a truth as a truth and a falsehood as a falsehood. Here, the question arises that if you have really committed a murder then you deserve the punishment. The punishment is certain to be given. After the verdict it so happens that the accused is sent behind the bars in the jail. Now, he has two options either he takes the punishment in his stride and finish his rest of the life in the jail. The second option is that he regrets. He brings change in his nature. He learns good habits by acting in this manner. These accused are providing sufficient material to the God. Now, look at the second picture. The accused was punished when he went to jail. He fought with the people there also. He ran away from the jail one day. Police apprehended him again and sent back him to the jail once again. This time he was punished not only for the crime, he did earlier but also for running away from the jail. In such a case, he will be severely punished. The law and judge can't do anything to help him. You will reap what you have sown. You have choice either take it in your stride or remain unhappy about it. It depends on you whether you remain unfair to people. You will have to change yourself.

Moral Values

Now, the point is whatever will be your *karmic* account you have to repay on this earth in this birth and lead a pure, divine and simple life. If you lean towards jealousy, anger, arrogance, incomplete desire, greed, sex and revengeful in that case God will use the same materials and create a new human being in their next berth. There is nothing in his hand. It is as simple as that whatever we provide to our Almighty, he re-creates us with the same raw materials in our subsequent berth.

You can't leave bad habits by going to temple and mosque. You have to control them. You will have to ask yourself time and again that why we have come in this world. Some people understand that they have come here to lead only a materialistic life. If you look at the history then you will find that scholars, thinkers, inventors and researchers have calculated that the existence of man has been on this earth for fourteen hundred crore years. The history of the development of this world is witness to the fact that we are developing everyday our purpose should be that we should progress regularly. As far as possible, it should be helpful to live comfortably. We also have to bring happiness and convenience in this life according to our ability. We have to earn knowledge and use it for welfare of all our ancestors has drawn a road map to live and acquire knowledge. We are using them everyday. It becomes our duty that we also contribute in it.

As *yoga Guru Swami* Ramdev spreads the moral education of *yoga* and its benefit in the world in view of enlightening the sufferers and sinners, who want to come out of this phase. The God has created you. No one should have any doubt about it. He, by bringing you in this world on the basis of your past life good work, gives you an opportunity. We waste this golden opportunity in every new life and take birth time and again if the man listens to the voice of his inner-soul and change his life accordingly then he can achieve great successes. The God bless the human being with many kinds of powers. Now, it depends on the man whether he uses those God-gifted powers in the right or wrong directions.

Do Good Things

Let us briefly discuss it. First, we talk about the physical power provided by the God. By keeping your body healthy we use our physical energy. You should do good things in the hope of achieving big and great feat through your perseverance. It is a divine boon and this physical energy of yours can be useful only when you remain honest and dealing fair and correct. If you act like this you will not feel scared and will not be worried. Your body will also remain free from disease. The God has blessed you with the power to create also. When you are born in this world then you are alone. Soon you get parents and siblings. After attaining maturity you get married and raise a family with children. This is the unique power which God has given to produce but some people think that their job is confined to producing children only and leave them at their own fate. It is your responsibility towards children that you must give them good culture and education to make them good human being but first you have to become noble and good human being yourself. You have to create a proper environment for them so that they can flourish and could be useful for family, society and nation. These are some of such responsibilities you should not be avoided at any circumstances to impart them among your children. You should use positively the power of these God-gifted qualities for a meaningful purpose.

Money Root Cause of Evils

If a human being listens to his inner-voice and act according to his choice then it is not possible that he will not succeed. Where there is success of money and wealth; we generally see the abuse of the power of money also. Money is the root cause of all evils. For getting more money we used to commit countless bad actions which would fatten our *karmic* account. With the same money, we can do countless good work as well. Such work will do a world of good to the welfare of the whole humanity, society and the nation. Now, it is up to you that which way you want to go? How to use the power of money given by the God in the right direction?

By adopting right direction for the cause of the society you will get new energy in bonus. For example, the power of self-respect. Please allow us to tell you the facts that if you can't respect yourself can't get respect from others. By this power of self-respect you can undertake any big job. You will earn a rightful place in the society. People will respect you. You will get a respectable position in the society. Beware that we don't discriminate against anybody and can not be unfair to others.

We don't have to forget this simple thing that we have to improve ourselves gradually day by day. We have to make our brain and mind to work in unison. We have to increase our knowledge by studying different good books for the purpose getting knowledgeable in turn our self-confidence will go up. Those who are confident personified in their respective field they are more successful. We have to find that by getting good education and doing deep-thinking and through knowledge we can bring peace in our families to make our life happier and enjoyable.

Often wrong notions have been spreaded for thousands of years that a human being becomes a dog, a cat or another animal after this life on the basis of his past bad deeds. Such confusing notions have made people a victim of misunderstanding. Let us clear that a human being will always reborn as a human. In your day to day life, you get a plant of tamarind by sowing a seed of tamarind. If you will plant mango you will get mango. This is part of nature. This is how the world moves. Therefore, accept it that human will be re-born as a human only.

As we have mentioned earlier that human being has been existed here for forteen-hundred crore years. You will be surprise to know that we originated from mere a cell and today our body has fifteen lakh crore cells. It is necessary that these cells are our good friends and react according to your deed. When you do anything wrong then these cells react with each other and leave a bad impact on your body. If they will be friend you will not be disturbed, therefore man has to do a lot of activities after being re-born. He has to acquire lot of knowledge. He has to surrender his life to the service of humanity, let's discuss for a while that how many times a man is born?

Cycle of Life

The man is born from the womb of his mother. Automatically, mother's body is a biological birth. It is physical birth also as we have already said it earlier. Usually we have witnessed if an infant doesn't get due love and affection from his family God knows what would have happened to him. An infant is just like a toy for the whole family as the child grows, he starts learning and understanding from the environment. Gradually his action and language becomes more acceptable as he starts using his brain and his mind also starts developing slowly. All the researches have established that the total development of mind is completed by the time the child is five years old. You can say it is the mental birth of a man from that stage.

The third kind of birth is a maturity birth as such the birth of judgement in mind and brain. It is that kind of birth when a man starts to make distinction what is wrong and what is right. The birth of maturity gives a new direction to the man. It inspires the man who does biggest jobs on the strength of his courage and ability in life. Generally, when a man is born he accomplishes something extraordinarily by virtue of his own effort and endeavour.

Then comes the turn of authentic birth. In this birth, a man ideas, behaviour, nature dialect and language become authentic. This authentic birth born out on the basis of gaining experience and knowledge giving a solid identity to a man.

After playing long innings, a man gets another birth it is called conscious birth; by this stage a kind of consciousness in the form of good behaviour, ideas, nature, business and dealings have developed to transform him into a a new man. All these births we are talking about of a man have nothing to do with his age.

Divine Birth

In the final analysis comes the divine birth of a man. When the divine birth takes place then he comes out of the grip from all the bad activities like jealousies, affections, goodness and evils. He achieves such a mental state where he experiences extreme peace and tranquility. He feels blessed and contented by this divine birth.

In this chapter, we discussed about the birth of a mankind in detail. The secret of human birth in the world is such a unique incident lies at the hands of God only. Today science might have progressed by leaps and bound but no machine, no factory no industry has been so far able to create a human being. It depends solely upon your *karma*. So, we can draw a conclusion from these discussions that how to use and in which job this beautiful body has to be utilised this decision has confined to your good activities and too in the present berth.

11

The Soul and Our Healthy Life

Dishonesty

Today the biggest concern of the people is their pain and sufferings. They are suffering from various dreaded diseases like cancer, diabetes, blood pressure and heart-attack etc. People are even suffering from such type of diseases which have got no treatment available in the medical science and people hardly aware of the bad consequences of these unknown diseases. Today people are bound to live a sick and unhappy life due to their ignorance to a great extent. In fact, because of their sickness they can not eat and drink properly. No matter how much money they have but because of their illness they cannot enjoy the charm of life in right spirit. It is a known fact that the body which is sick cannot do anything in a correct way. Have you ever thought why man is surrounded by such illness? Why he is suffering from various known and unknown diseases? The biggest reason is that the people are not honest in their profession, business and personal dealing with others at the time of doing their job.

Today we see a man can harm anybody for his own benefit. Greed, craving for liquor, smoke, sex, jealousy and dishonest behaviour are leading him to cheat people.

Nobody is accepting this fact that his dealing with people is not correct. He thinks whatever he does is correct and others are wrong. With this approach and dishonest behaviour you can get temporary benefit and its far-sighted results are equally dangerous. They know it by very well that this is not right but in spite of they refuse to budge. They don't mind to do wrong with others. We have found two reasons: one, they think that when the whole world is doing it then what is wrong in doing it. The second reason is that they think whatever wrong they would do to people, later they will go to temple and pray to God for forgiving them. To cover their wrong doings they used to perfrom *Pooja* or *Bhandara* to please God. It is their belief that they will keep on doing wrong to others and the God will spare them for their doing *pujas and bhandara.*

Will they get peace by doing all these worldly things by leading their life according to their whims and fancies? Will they get any big achievement in their life? Can God give them a guarantee they would not suffer from any kind of disease. If God could have done this miracle then no one would have fallen ill. Today the situation is totally opposite. A large number of people are sick and even beds in the hospitals are not available to treat them. Hospitals are full of patients who are suffering from various type of diseases and few also might have counting their last breath. Just think who are these people? Are they common man? Are they poor and labourer class ? Surprisingly, you will find the people who got admitted in these hospitals are mostly from the rich and affluent sections. They are kept themselves alive only with the help of medicines and injections. If hospitals stopped to provide them treatment they will not be able to survive very long.

You will be surprise to know that man is the best creation of God but here the biggest question comes why he is suffering so badly from pain and sickness? Why his mind and body are not working in unison to get out of these problems ?

Pehla Sukh

We know very well that the main happiness comes from our healthy body as there is general saying "Only healthy body has a healthy mind". It is said '*Pehla sukh nirogi kaya*' means if we will maintain our good health then everything will be taken care of. A healthy heart and sharp brain develops only in healthy body. But you have to control your heart and mind that can get affected from your own environment. Your polluted thought with anger play a negative impact on others. Your deceitful, cunning mentality first attacks you physically it attacks your brain and do harm your body badly from inside. You may become sick and tired because of that. If you lead a pure and pious life your body will have in a process of self-generating and curable mode. Even incurable diseases will get cured itself. Mr Malhotra is one such exampleas all his diseases such as diabetes and blood pressure were cured by himself without any doctors and medicine help. He cured himself through meditation, spiritual guidance and having pure food and healthy thoughts.

Now, the question arises that the God has given you a healthy body but because of your unhealthy environment and poor background you polluted your mind easily which can make a bad impact on your heart, mind, and brain. You will find so many people saying that I have done this out of jealousy or for getting easy money. You know it is wrong but you keep on doing these and lead a unhealthy life.

Supreme Power

Mostly people are unaware about that there is a 'supreme power' who controls the human life. That is God. Generally, when people think about God they think about temples and mosque. Most of them are not aware about the element of God which itself exists inside them. It is understood if God is ominipresent and ominipotent it must be in you also. That divine element is only 'soul'.

Why can't we identify that? We cannot identify our soul which is within us due to our ignorance. It gives a feeling that we are leading a healthy life, our heart and mind are so dominant that we forget about our 'soul' completely. It is interesting to know that without the soul there is nothing in life then why we ignore it? We should listen to our soul and follow its instructions properly.

The God has created our body and its nature of natural working ability. It works automatically. The supreme power has given us the ability to treat everything in proper way. If, we imbibe the spirit of high-thinking and follow good practices like *yoga,* meditation, keep weekly fast and know the importance of sound sleep in our life then we can cure our body automatically. You will get so many examples on this earth to prove that our body has the capacity and ability to cure itself.

Just think who cures fishes in the oceans? Who cures wild animals in the forest on this earth? They cure themselves and they have got capacity to re-generate their body parts also. Likewise, you can also cure yourself and re-generate your body parts. There are various kinds of immune systems are already existed in our body itself. The medicine like blood and bones could not be produce in any factory though we have made progress remarkably in medical science. You need to correct your mental behaviour, food habits and need to become a self-confident person. You need to give right direction to your body cells to co-operate with each other. It will be only possible when you will be clear and honest in your dealing with your body and lead an ideal life.

12

Conclusion

Soul Leaves in Universe

Now, the point is who will break the ice? Who will tell the importance of soul in our life? It is small effort and contribution from our side that people should get to know about their soul and get peace and happiness in their life. Soul has its own power and identity. It is infinite, mature, eternal, and divine. It guides to attain purity and ultimate *Moksha.* It is debatable that what comes first, body or soul? According to our understanding soul is permanent and it selects its body according to its requirement and mental attitude. That is how we get our new body, home and wealth. It is also a debatable that where soul goes and lives after leaving the body. If we believe in super natural power then we should believe that soul leaves in universe.

The whole universe is controlled by almighty God. That is why we say his presence is everywhere. But you will surprise to know as far as the human being's cycle and recycle is concern nothing is in his hand. What you gave him he makes you accordingly and sends you on this earth again. You have already read this in detail in previous chapters. It's like you watch television at home. It needs electricity to switch on and after that it's your wish that what kind of programmes you would like to watch. Television is an example of God it has everything but it doesn't do anything by itself until you switch on your TV set. The moment you connect your TV set with electricity you start watching programmes. Just imagine for a moment this electricity is your soul. In television you get to see different kinds of channels. Now it is your choice what kind of programme you would like to see. It's like there are too many things in this materialistic world around you. God has created this world. You take birth on this earth and interact with various kinds of people. You encounter with lot of good and bad situations. People respond in their own manner. Though God has created this entire world but he is not coming and doing anything. That is you who are doing everything on this earth and interacting with this world. Some times you meet bad people sometimes you come into contact with really nice people. You deal with people and people deal with you in their own manner. If you put a top angle camera and the Arial shot of this world then you will get to know how this world is interacting. It is up to you what is to be adopted and left. Television set will not give you anything though he has everything. It is up to you what you want to get from it.

As You Sow, So You Reap

You get the knowledge of it and how to identify your soul in previous chapters. We hope you must be cleared about the nature of soul and its power. If you start living with soul, act according to it after hearing soul's instructions, I am sure the things will be changed forever and started fall on your expected lines. It will help you to construct your life in a positive manner. Your thinking and foresight will widen your mental horizon and take a positive lead in life. This vision will give you a strong base to your wavering heart and mind. You will get constant peace in your life. It will stabilises your heart and mind and add creativity in your work. When you will be creative it will elevate your confidence and this confidence will help you to achieve higher success. With peace of mind, even you will enjoy working on unexplored areas such as corruption, innovation and education etc.

The soul will lead you towards honest and truthful way. It will generate self-confidence in you to face today's challenges. Your mature nature will take you to the greatness. With these qualities you will be able to express yourself freely in public. You will speak the truth without any hesitation and fear and will not be scared of life and death. No matter how old and young you are but with this nature you will always feel young and energetic. This is possible only through your soul-enlightenment.

By doing all this first you need to do commitment with yourself. If you can win yourself means you have achieved great success. These are the foundation of life. It brings common vision, dedication and discipline to human life and life becomes enjoyable and meaningful and purposeful.

No action will happen without God will. On the contrary, we also say that what you will reap that you sow. Both the statements are contradictory but true to a great extent. The almighty God has created everything including human being. But it is your deed which will solely determine your fate. You can reap a rich harvest by imbibing the spirit of goodness and *vice versa*.